Dealing Wit`
In A Week

Naomi Langford-Wood and Brian Salter have experienced difficult people across five continents, and their books on dealing with difficult people have sold over 50,000 copies. Brian now works for China Central TV in Beijing, and Naomi is a consultant based in England.

Dealing With Difficult People In A Week

Naomi Langford-Wood and Brian Salter

Teach® Yourself

First published in Great Britain in 1998 by Hodder Education. An Hachette UK company.

This edition published in 2016 by John Murray Learning

British Library Cataloguing in Publication Data: a catalogue record for this title is available from the British Library.

ISBN: 978 1 473 60778 1

eISBN: 978 1 444 15885 4

1

Typeset by Cenveo® Publisher Services.

Printed and bound in Great Britain by CPI Group (UK) Ltd, Croydon, CR0 4YY.

John Murray Learning policy is to use papers that are natural, renewable and recyclable products and made from wood grown in sustainable forests. The logging and manufacturing processes are expected to conform to the environmental regulations of the country of origin.

John Murray Learning
Carmelite House
50 Victoria Embankment
London EC4Y 0DZ
www.hodder.co.uk

Contents

Introduction

Dealing with difficult people can be very demoralizing. It can upset your state of mind, your sense of purpose and your prospective achievement. Difficult people may be encountered just about anywhere, both in business and in everyday life. They are frequently to be met where stress can lead normally reasonable people into being rude, impatient or acting emotionally – and sometimes a combination of all three. Many difficult people do not realize they are behaving badly, while others systematically behave so because it makes them feel they have the upper hand in our lives.

Perhaps more than anywhere else, learning to handle difficult people in the workplace can result in getting the best out of them and, by extension, the best from ourselves, as well as making for a more pleasant atmosphere. Learning about what may make these people behave in a difficult way and being able to moderate their behaviour can reduce our stress levels and allow us to operate more effectively.

As difficult people rarely see themselves as such, they are most unlikely to think that they should read this book. Although we have referred to 'he' throughout this text, this is for the sake of ease and continuity and is not intended to infer that men are more likely to be difficult people than women.

You can learn about a different aspect of the subject on every day of the week:

On Sunday we look at understanding ourselves better, which gives us the potential to improve our self-image. In so doing, we are more likely to be able to resist the words and actions of difficult people.

On Monday we consider different styles of behaviour and, while there are many, almost every one may be attributable to just three categories. If we can understand someone's behaviour, even if we don't approve of it, we have a chance of coping with it and even working with it.

On Tuesday we learn about coping with different problem people. In looking at some of the more common types of behaviour, we can consider how we might respond to the personality displayed in order to manage the behaviour we find difficult.

On Wednesday we learn about managing conflict situations at work, and especially when dealing with clients. While conflict is usual, it is not inevitable and we can manage it to achieve positive results. Making the most of a logical approach and minimizing our emotional response helps us cope better with conflict.

On Thursday we are shown that everything we have already learned is supported and enhanced by our basic communication skills and body language. These can help reduce the possibility of misunderstandings or ambiguity. Our non-verbal signals may reinforce what we are saying, or assist our understanding of another's viewpoint.

On Friday we look at how to say no and how to deal with difficult clients. We see that, when appropriate, saying no can be constructive and we learn how to use this technique effectively.

On Saturday, the strands of the previous six days are all pulled together, emphasizing that each topic builds on and informs the others. You're in control now!

SUNDAY

Understanding yourself

From the moment we are born and for the whole of our lives, we interact with different people. Some of these interactions are easy, others less so. Today we look at why some people with whom we come into contact are not easy to deal with, leading us to think of them as difficult people. We need to think about the possible causes of their behaviour, to allow us to respond to it appropriately.

To understand other people, it is necessary first to try to understand ourselves. Communication is, after all, a two-way process; therefore how we respond to a person we find challenging will have an effect on their behaviour and on the outcome of the interaction. This is why we should take both our own self-image and the perception others have of us into account.

Today we will look at various scenarios that show how a conversation may have different outcomes according to the words and tone of voice we use. They reveal how our own reactions to the behaviour of a difficult person are instrumental in shaping the interaction with them.

Defining 'difficult people'

We should perhaps begin by defining what we mean by the term 'difficult people'. When you interact with someone, the process is essentially two-way. Just as you will respond to the words and actions of another person, so he will do the same to you. To really understand yourself takes courage, because there are always things that we do not like about ourselves and which we would prefer to hide from our appraisal of our strengths and weaknesses.

Over time, from the day we are born, we all get to learn what is expected in our behavioural patterns to elicit the best responses from those with whom we are having a dialogue. At birth, a simple yowl is usually sufficient to get mum to come rushing forward to feed us, clean us and give us a cuddle. Effectively, then, we are taught from birth that when we demand something noisily enough, we get what we want or need.

As we get older, however, we learn pretty rapidly that it is a question not just of getting the meaning of the words right, but also of the expressions that go with those words, the epithets that add politeness, respect, or whatever feelings we want to go with them, and the gestures that can also accompany such a dialogue.

The patterns of our personality are set very early on in childhood. Events and other people will have caused us to grow up the way we have, with the self-doubts and prejudices that we all possess. The way in which our mothers and fathers treated us, for example, will have had a profound effect on our sense of self-worth. It is all too easy (and all too sad) for the most well-meaning adult to inflict all kinds of mental scars on his children. Being overprotective, for example, can lead a child to become over-reliant on others to fight his battles for him, leaving him with little sense of self-worth. Most parents do only what they think is best at the time and it is a great shock to them that something they regarded as insignificant, and perhaps have all but forgotten, was a monstrous milestone in the life of their child.

SUNDAY

MONDAY

TUESDAY

WEDNESDAY

THURSDAY

FRIDAY

SATURDAY

SIBLING RIVALRY WHEN HE WAS A KID

By holding back on displays of affection, an adult can lead a child into believing that he is unworthy of such love; by telling a child he is stupid or that his brother or sister is 'better' than him, an adult can cause that child to do everything in so half-hearted a fashion that eventually it becomes a self-fulfilling prophecy.

Someone who has had an unsettled childhood can also suffer in later life from being unable to form positive relationships with others. The effect of this is that he feels inadequate and inferior to his peers. And so we have a potential ever-decreasing spiral of self-image in the making, the behaviour pattern of which is very difficult to jettison in adulthood.

These feelings of inadequacy translate into everyday behaviour and actions. We are all a product of our upbringing. When you next encounter a bullying type, instead of reacting by thinking, 'What have I done to deserve this?' ask yourself what kind of an upbringing he might have had. Does he feel inadequate as a person, and are his bullying tactics perhaps a cover for the way he feels about himself? Ask yourself also why you have reacted in that manner – what is it about your inner self and sense of self-worth that makes that your first reaction?

Why are people difficult?

When we talk about dealing with difficult people, what we really mean is dealing with difficult behaviour. By learning to understand what it is that makes someone else behave and talk in a difficult way, we are in a better position not only to take charge of the situation but also to help the other person resolve the conflicts that made him or her 'difficult' in the first place.

Unfortunately, the natural way in which many of us react when we meet a difficult person is often more inclined to make that person's behaviour even more difficult. Ask yourself if you have ever reacted to someone by:

- sharply answering back
- becoming defensive rather than dealing with the problematical issue
- ignoring the meaning of what they are saying because you are so annoyed with the way they have spoken to you
- feeling confused and frightened
- becoming speechless with rage
- becoming unable to think of anything else at the time.

It is likely that you will have experienced each of these reactions on numerous occasions. Many of us react in ways that make the problem worse, because we are reacting rather than thinking first. Yet, by stopping and thinking things through from the other person's perspective, by controlling the way we feel and attempting to act calmly and completely rationally, we can benefit in a number of ways:

- We will feel more in control of ourselves and our own destiny, as well as the situation as a whole.
- By reducing our emotional reactions, we will be better able to think clearly and objectively.
- We will feel less hampered by frustration or anger.
- We will feel better about ourselves for not having responded like with like.

So ask yourself – and be honest – do you let others dictate the way you feel about yourself? Turned round the other way, do you think your moods or actions could affect the behaviour

SUNDAY
MONDAY
TUESDAY
WEDNESDAY
THURSDAY
FRIDAY
SATURDAY

and actions of another person? Depending on your current state of mind, this may or may not be easy to answer. If you feel considerably discomforted by the potential grasping of the truth, then it might be a good idea to leave this until you have reflected overnight. An honest appraisal of this now is vital to getting to grips with other people and their difficult behaviour – and how you are going to be able to cope with it better.

Let's face it, persuading a difficult person to become good-natured and easy to deal with is not something that you can achieve instantly – if at all. It may be that, in time, you can make him appreciate how unreasonable his behaviour is and get him to change his ways. Over the short term, if you cannot change him, then maybe the next best thing is to change the way you react to him. After all, it is invariably the recipient of his behaviour who gets hurt or demoralized, rather than the difficult person himself.

TIP *The key to coping with a difficult person lies in understanding that person.*

Communication: a two-way process

All communication is a series of reactions and counter-reactions, if you think about it. Your difficult person will react to what you say or write – and to your body language – in the same way as you will react to what he says. But if your reaction is different from what he is expecting, it is possible to break the cycle – to get him to counter-react in a different way from the way he was expecting to do – and very often this has the effect of defusing the unpleasant situation and improving communication between the two of you. It can happen very fast.

Everyone reacts to awkwardness in a different way. It's not surprising when you consider that some people might be shy and retiring while others are extrovert and apparently over-confident. By making others feel low and bad about themselves, insecure people can give themselves a boost by inwardly telling themselves that they are better than others. By giving in to a bully, for instance, all you are doing is letting him win. But by responding in a calm and collected way, you can influence the way he counter-reacts to you, and often it is possible to do this without him even knowing.

Think about how you usually react to a difficult person. Do you normally answer back sharply to someone who needles you? Although perfectly natural, this response is hardly likely to improve the situation, except that in the short term you might feel better for being able to get your feelings off your chest. But what have you achieved? Difficult people are so used to behaving in a particular way and leading their victims to react to them in such a way that they can then 'move in for the kill', that by denying them the wherewithal to play their trump card, you have effectively got the better of them. By not responding in a 'natural' way, you can break the cycle that your antagonist has set up for you to fall into. If you neither cower before a bullying manager, nor angrily explode at a subordinate, you effectively deny him the inner satisfaction of his own personal superiority factor; and when difficult behaviour no longer works, most such antagonists fall back into a more reasonable frame of mind – what else can they do?

Suppose that one of your clients shouts at you and creates a row about something that was clearly not your fault. (Many people staffing telephone help desks get this kind of treatment on a regular basis.) You can respond in a number of ways. For instance, you could:

- defend both yourself and your company
- be calm and identify the real problem
- concentrate on his problem rather than on your own feelings, recognizing that the client is angry with the present situation – not with you. There is therefore no need to defend yourself.

The first response is likely to satisfy neither you nor your client. So why do it? You are simply allowing yourself to become the punchbag of your frustrated client. But if you concentrate on his problem rather than your own feelings, as in the second and third alternatives, the client is more likely to end up in a positive frame of mind and think better of both you and your company.

Frankly, the customer is not interested in who made the mistake in the first place. All he wants is the problem to be resolved and he is frustrated as well as anxious about whether the company will take his problem seriously; and you will stay calmer if you don't become defensive. In short, both sides win.

So by taking a moment to reflect before you react, especially if you know that this person is difficult to deal with anyway, you have a much better chance of coming out on top. Simply having a shouting match brings you down to his level and achieves nothing at all – and it potentially creates a stalemate situation, which is even more difficult to resolve.

Similarly, if one of your fellow workers shouts at you, for whatever reason, which of the following scenarios is most likely to be conducive to a healthy outcome?

- You fly into a rage and tell him what you think of him.
- You pause and tell him in a calm and controlled manner that you feel angry about what he has just said.

The first scenario is almost guaranteed to get him to scream back at you, which will mean that neither of you will take the slightest notice of what the other is saying, regardless of the truth of what either of you is saying. The second scenario, on the other hand, is far more assertive and, by controlling your emotions, you will also be much more likely to get your point of view across.

If this person has a reputation for being difficult generally, it should also help that you know instinctively that it is not really you who is being attacked. Admittedly, it can still be pretty unpleasant being on the receiving end of such behaviour, but at least you can hold your head up knowing that if anyone is inadequate, he is. You therefore also need to identify and then come to terms with the impact your behaviour has on others – good or bad.

The classic example

How often have you been driving along a road when some inconsiderate motorist overtakes a whole stream of cars on a bend and all but causes an collision in the process? It is, unfortunately, all too common an experience these days. The natural reaction of many is one of fury: to swear at the careless driver and to fume at all inconsiderate motorists. But, in the process, your concentration lapses and your driving may suffer as a consequence. And the corollary of this is that other people then sound their horns because they are suffering from the bad driving of someone else. Meanwhile, the original driver who caused all the problems in the first place is miles away, probably upsetting yet more people at that very moment.

In this case, the ones to suffer are the 'victims' of that first bad driver. Anger would have been the perfectly natural reaction, but it has achieved nothing except to allow the actions of someone else to affect their feelings and judgement.

In the same way, if you allow yourself to become stressed at the behaviour of others, don't be surprised if the one to suffer most is you. Not only will you fail to get an adequate response from your antagonists, but you will, more than likely, be the one left feeling exhausted and emotionally drained.

Feeling inadequate

But getting angry with difficult people is not the only harmful way of reacting to them. It is just as bad if you don't stand up to them or if you make excuses and become defensive. Think what you are saying to them with these kinds of responses. 'You're probably right and I'm really the one in the wrong.' Is that what you want to convey?

And what about feelings of negativity? Suppose you are due to go for an interview and you spend the week beforehand thinking of all the reasons why you might not get the job or be put in charge of that project. Think about it: not only may your feelings of negativity cause you to see the worst in every situation, but they will also cause others to see the negative aspects of you. Rest assured, then, that if you go into the interview in this frame of mind, you will certainly not convey the best impression to the interviewer, thus confirming your worst fears to your inner self. And worse still, the entire week may have been ruined by your fear of the unknown.

Case study

We know of one married couple who were going through a difficult patch, who every night wrote out a 'disaster diary' of everything that had gone wrong that day. It didn't matter how small or how annoying the 'disaster' was; everything was entered into that book. The wonderful thing was that when they read a given entry the following day or the next week or whenever, what had at the time appeared to be something dreadful became in time totally insignificant. The effect was that their marriage improved dramatically, and the feelings of negativity, which had at one time appeared to hover over them like a black cloud, simply evaporated.

Now think things through the opposite way round. Begin by making up a list of all the bad things that have happened to you this week. Study it well and ask yourself whether any of these things would have happened anyway, without you there. Now make a list of all the good things that have recently happened to you and all the good characteristics you can boast of. Doesn't that put it all into perspective?

What do others think of you?

We have so far talked about the reactions we have to difficult people. But have you ever really stopped to think about how others see you? It's all too easy to think that the way we see ourselves is the same as the way others see us. In fact, the opposite is much closer to the truth. Perhaps you believe it is important to say what you are thinking, regardless of the consequences. But how would you feel if someone treated you in the same way? In causing others distress through the things you say, you are then no different from the difficult person you endured before. How will others, then, regard you? The likelihood is that they will turn away from you, and you will end up feeling isolated. And it will be your own fault entirely. Don't be surprised, then, if this leads you into more negativity in the way you treat others, so that your behaviour gives cause for concern.

How can we change?

Despite our upbringing and the effect that parents and other mentors have had on us, the fact is that the way we think of ourselves is not some immovable concept cast in stone. The great thing to realize is that we can actually choose to change our self-image.

We all have mini-disasters in our lives. Perhaps none are so public as those of professional sportspeople competing in international competitions. Even the best champion ice-skaters fall over; Premier League footballers miss easy goals; and many a great cricketer has chided himself for being bowled out. But they all realize that nothing is served by punishing oneself after the event. The ice-skater gets up and carries on; the footballer concentrates on lining up another goal; and as for the cricketer – well, there is always another day!

It is only worth looking back at one's failures if there is a lesson to be learned from them. And if you do learn from a mistake, it can be regarded as something positive – not something to be ashamed of. So leave your failures behind you where they belong: in the past.

In the same way, you should try to build on your successes. Make a mental list of everything you like about yourself. Even if you feel you are in the depths of depression, there is always something that you can find to put on that list if you think hard enough. People who have a poor image of themselves, for instance, often think that they can think of nothing good to say. The truth is, however, that such people are often highly sensitive and tend to be kind and compassionate. If those characteristics applied to a stranger that you met, you would react positively to them. So react positively to yourself and continue the list in that vein.

TIP *Try listing the good things that have happened to you throughout your life. Everyone has successes, however small. Recall how good you felt when you had achieved those successes.*

By learning to improve your self-image, you are more likely to be able to resist the damaging words and actions of difficult people; and by gaining a better insight into yourself you will automatically gain an insight into the way others act and speak; you may even begin to understand why they are acting the way they are; and once you can begin to feel pity for someone, however dreadful a person he is, you will find that you no longer feel hurt by the things he says to you.

Later in this book, you will learn the techniques of how to deal with all manner of difficult people in a variety of situations. By learning to deal with their moods and their own feelings of inadequacy, you will be more likely to succeed in coping with them and turn a potentially negative situation into one that will prove to be positive for both parties.

Summary

The key factor in dealing successfully with difficult people is to understand what makes them behave in the way they do. Furthermore, we are likely to be able to manage the words and actions of difficult people if our own self-image is positive. We have seen that the foundations of our personalities formed in childhood influence the behaviour of those we find difficult as well as our own responses to them.

We have learned that perception of self-worth is often a main constituent of people's personalities, but by changing our self-image we can become more successful in dealing with difficult people. Many of us react to an awkward situation in ways that can make a problem worse, but it is possible to overcome this by pausing to consider the other person's perspective and to control the way we feel in order to act calmly and rationally.

SUNDAY
MONDAY
TUESDAY
WEDNESDAY
THURSDAY
FRIDAY
SATURDAY

Fact-check (answers at the back)

Some of these questions have more than one correct answer.

1. What is good communication?
a) A one-way process ❏
b) A two-way process ❏
c) More about speaking than listening ❏
d) A process in which speaking and listening are equally important ❏

2. What characterizes the patterns of our personality?
a) They are never fixed ❏
b) They become fixed during early adulthood ❏
c) They are set very early on in childhood ❏
d) They are set before we are born ❏

3. Why is it useful to understand why people behave and talk in a difficult way?
a) We are in a better position to take charge of the situation ❏
b) We can tell them exactly what they are doing wrong ❏
c) They can instantly improve their behaviour ❏
d) We can help them resolve the conflicts that made them 'difficult' ❏

4. How should we react when we meet a difficult person?
a) Defensively and emotionally ❏
b) Angrily ❏
c) By staying silent, otherwise we are encouraging the difficult behaviour ❏
d) Calmly ❏

5. How easily can we help a difficult person to become good-natured and easy to deal with?
a) It is not something you can achieve instantly – if at all ❏
b) It may be possible in time if you can make him appreciate that the behaviour is unreasonable ❏
c) It may be less easy than changing the way you react to him ❏
d) It will be straightforward, as the difficult person gets hurt and demoralized with each difficult interaction ❏

6. How can we change the course of a difficult communication?
a) It always follows a set pattern ❏
b) The course of the communication cannot be changed midway ❏
c) If your reaction is not as anticipated, it may break the cycle ❏
d) A different counter-reaction may defuse an unpleasant situation ❏

7. Why might someone exhibit bullying behaviour?
a) To hide their insecurities ❑
b) To give themselves a boost by making others feel low ❑
c) To dominate the conversation, whatever you do ❑
d) Out of frustration at a particular situation ❑

8. If a client shouts at you and verbally attacks you, which of the following are appropriate?
a) To meet strength with strength by shouting back; it's the only way to make him listen ❑
b) To defend both yourself and your company ❑
c) To be calm and identify the real problem ❑
d) To recognize that the client is angry with the situation, not with you personally ❑

9. What will help a difficult client?
a) For the problem to be resolved ❑
b) For the company to take his problem seriously ❑
c) For you to stay calm and not be defensive ❑
d) For you to agree with him, whatever he says ❑

10. If you allow yourself to become stressed at the difficult behaviour of others, who suffers?
a) No one ❑
b) Those around you ❑
c) The person with difficult behaviour ❑
d) You ❑

Different styles of behaviour

Today we consider different styles of behaviour. Initially it may seem as though we might apply any number of different labels to personality types, but the vast majority can be categorized more simply into just three types. When dealing with difficult people it is important to be able to recognize the type of behaviour exhibited, as it will allow you to deal with it, or even work with it.

The three main categories into which each behavioural style may be assigned are passive, aggressive and assertive. Full descriptions follow for each of these three personality types, including day-to-day characteristics, leading on to examples of experiences such a person is likely to have. Explanations are given of how each personality type is likely to feel about themselves, followed by descriptions of the feelings likely to be aroused in those who have to deal with them.

When we understand the style of the behaviour, we are in a better position to anticipate the type of interaction we are likely to have and therefore to respond appropriately. We learn that, in order to help ourselves and others, it is beneficial to move oneself towards the assertive style.

Categories of behavioural style

When we talk about the different styles of behaviour of individuals, it is easy to use an almost limitless number of descriptions. For instance, people may be described as ogres, wimps or bullies, or as lecherous, uncaring, dominating and so on. Yet, when you think of it, almost every behavioural style can be subsumed into one of three main categories:

1 Passive
2 Aggressive
3 Assertive

When dealing with difficult people, it is important to be able to recognize the signs they are exhibiting and to see these for what they are. That way, you can minimize the effects they have on you, for it is a truism that you can really only expect to influence others when you can see them as they are rather than as they would wish to be portrayed, or as you wish they were. Understanding someone's behaviour does not necessarily imply that you approve of it, but it does mean that you can cope with it, at worst, and work with it, at best.

 Recognizing the personality type of difficult people enables us to deal more successfully with them.

Passive behaviour

Passive behaviour is most typified by people who put other people's needs before their own. While on the one hand this can be an attractive trait in some, it can also show that they have little respect for themselves, especially when they are reluctant to stand up for their rights. The result is that they are often put upon by others, even by those who are not normally aggressive.

The passive person is usually pretty insecure and will often show signs of an inferiority complex. Just as he has little respect for his own abilities and will often talk down his gifts, his own feelings of inadequacy are reinforced every time he meets an aggressive type, and he is more likely to take criticism as justified without stopping to consider if that is in fact the case. He will often accept the criticism, and only at a later date question its validity. The passive person is therefore often frustrated by his own inability to be assertive.

This hapless individual is also likely to be angry with himself, since he can see how others take advantage of him; yet he is unlikely to do anything to improve the situation as he sincerely believes that others will not take him seriously. This, in turn, causes him to experience even greater feelings of inadequacy, and the whole situation becomes a vicious circle.

In summary, a passive person is likely to feel:

- angry, because he knows only too well that others are ready to take advantage of him and he finds it difficult not to let them
- anxious, because he feels he is not in control of his own destiny
- negative, because he feels that, whatever he does, he is unlikely to get his way
- insecure, because he lacks self-confidence and is afraid of trying out anything new since he 'knows' instinctively that he will fail anyway

- frustrated, because he believes he cannot get his own way
- withdrawn, because no one 'wants to listen to him'
- lacking in energy, because everything he does is to satisfy someone else's desires rather than his own.

Until quite recently, it was considered normal for women to adopt a passive role – it was even expected. They 'knew their place' and kowtowed to their menfolk who held on to a traditional belief that their role was to be strong, to be the hunter, the breadwinner, the dominant partner in a marriage and to make the important decisions in any relationship. Strangely, it was also thought that men had more brain power and that women were emotionally unstable, too. Only in recent years, especially in Western societies, has this attitude been shaken to its very foundations as sexual equality has started to follow in the wake of the sixties' revolution, with women taking responsibility for both their bodies and their lifestyles, and they have learned to become more assertive in their behaviour.

Men, however, have had to start to unlearn their previously understood role of being the dominant gender, especially in the workplace, and to exhibit more of the caring and feeling sides of their personalities.

The descriptions of passive behaviour above may appear at first reading to be extreme, and to an extent this is indeed the case; however, although the degree of passivity may vary, such people are all around us.

Now, wouldn't your first reaction on meeting such a person be one of sympathy for him and a desire to help him boost his confidence? Well, unless you were a natural aggressor, you might well feel that. However, it is remarkable that after a very short time, the majority of those trying to help can end up feeling annoyed with the person for not trying to stand up for himself. This in turn can lead to an aggressive attitude towards that person because he has all but invited others to lose any kind of respect for him, and so they end up treating him the way he has come to expect to be treated!

When you try to compliment a passive person, he will often reject what you say. For instance, if you were to comment

SUNDAY

MONDAY

TUESDAY

WEDNESDAY

THURSDAY

FRIDAY

SATURDAY

favourably on his tie, he might well respond that he has had it for ages, rather than accepting the compliment in the spirit in which it is given. It can, indeed, be quite tiring to cope with someone who is so negative in everything he does and says, and it can also cause us to feel guilty because we can feel responsible for that person being taken advantage of. Because of this, many of us will avoid passive, negative people, which only acts to shore up their feelings of inadequacy.

So just as passive people feel bad about themselves, when we are dealing with passive people we can feel:

- annoyed, because we wish they would just stand up for themselves occasionally
- worn out, because we feel we are wasting valuable energy dealing with our own negative reactions to such behaviour
- superior, because we have lost respect for someone who is unwilling to stand up for himself
- withdrawn, because such a negative attitude undermines our own positive attitude
- negative, because of the amount of time needed to boost the passive person's ego before beginning to do the work or task in hand.

Aggressive behaviour

Aggressive behaviour can best be summed up as satisfying one's own needs at the expense of others'. Such a person is often a verbal bully who enjoys a feeling of power over other people. But just as physical bullying is often the outward manifestation of someone who is cowardly by nature, oddly enough, aggressive behaviour is often the result of feelings of inadequacy and lack of self-worth. In that respect, aggressive behaviour is the classic bedfellow of the passive-behaviour person.

Aggressive people are also, as often as not, lonely. Their behaviour results in others shunning them, both in their personal lives and at work. They are so busy reassuring themselves that they are the best that they end up being overly critical of others. Nothing is ever their fault, and by extension, anything that goes wrong is due to someone else. Their lack of self-esteem does not allow them to admit faults. People who exhibit aggressive tendencies often feel:

- energetic, except that their energy is often destructive rather than constructive
- powerful, because they enjoy having others rush around carrying out their orders
- somewhat guilty, since they know they take advantage of others
- lonely, because their aggression alienates them from other people
- that they are always right, and that they have a monopoly of good ideas
- threatened, in case others might see through the veneer of outward confidence
- exasperated by the passive people who don't share their energy and speed.

Some people are inclined to mistake aggression for strength and act accordingly, in the belief that if they show others a 'soft underbelly', they will be regarded as weak. But such behaviour is more inclined to have the reverse effect on others, who may feel angry or frustrated because they might be powerless to do anything about it. For instance, if a manager behaves aggressively to a subordinate, the latter may be fearful of losing his job if he tells his boss exactly what he thinks of him. The 'victim' will therefore be resentful of the way in which he has been treated, but the aggressor may not even realize that he has caused such feelings in the subordinate. The end result is one of a breakdown in communication, with a resulting lack of efficiency and with neither party understanding where 'things have gone wrong'. In these cases it can be an uphill struggle to rescue the situation once the patterns of behaviour have been established.

People who exhibit aggressive behaviour can cause us to feel:

- defensive, because we feel that anything we do will be attacked unfairly
- resentful, because the aggressor appears to wield power unfairly

SUNDAY

MONDAY

TUESDAY

WEDNESDAY

THURSDAY

FRIDAY

SATURDAY

- threatened, because we resent such tactics
- humiliated, because no one likes to be made a fool of
- frustrated, because we are always having to be on the defensive
- withdrawn, because we try to avoid possible confrontations with the aggressor.

Those who deal regularly with an aggressive person are inclined to suffer high levels of stress, and this can have a damaging effect on their wellbeing. The aggressor, on the other hand, enjoys his apparent feelings of power since it appears to boost his authority. The result is that people tend to avoid aggressors if they possibly can, which in turn leads the latter to believe they are somehow special. And this makes them act even more aggressively, and once again we have a vicious circle.

Assertive behaviour

Assertive behaviour is the third category of behaviour described at the start of this chapter. The assertive person is concerned not only for his own rights and opinions, but also for the rights and opinions of others. In trying to obtain a win–win situation with others, the assertive person is willing to make compromises in a positive way, at the same time arguing his corner for what he passionately believes in.

Because respect plays an important part in the assertive person's attitude, it engenders respect in the attitudes of others with whom he is in daily contact, encouraging them to co-operate with him as fully as possible. This in itself produces a healthy atmosphere, in which creative work can be carried out and where people know that others appreciate their work. All in all, this then leads everyone to do their level best to perform even better, whatever the job in hand.

An assertive person is also one who is able to understand his own feelings and can impart how he feels to others. The trick is to be able to explain what you feel in such a way that you will not cause others to resent what you say. The reality is that people are much more comfortable knowing where they stand, even if there is implied criticism of their position, rather than having to guess at the real meaning behind the words.

Being assertive means you can be proud of your successes; but equally it means that you are not conceited about your achievements. It also means that you can learn from your mistakes, that no one has a monopoly on good ideas and that others can catch the enthusiasm that is such a characteristic of the assertive person.

Are you assertive?

People who can best be described as assertive often exhibit the following tendencies:

● They approach new tasks in a positive frame of mind.
● They are enthusiastic in their approach.
● They are honest in dealing with others.
● They are energetic, and direct that energy into reaching their goals.
● They have good communication skills with others.
● They are willing to take risks, but at the same time they know their own limitations.
● They understand that other people have needs and feelings just as they do.

Assertive people are generally the ones other people most like to be associated with. Because they are not seen as manipulative, people work easily with them. Because their behaviour is consistent, communication by whatever medium is open and trusted. Regular communication lets others know what is expected of them, and so the whole team is able to turn its energies to achieving goals rather than infighting.

When dealing with assertive people, others are most likely to feel positive because:

- they sense that their success is a shared success
- they know where they stand
- they can reciprocate feelings of respect
- they can direct their energies into constructive areas
- they feel they can trust you and respond to your positive influence by helping you
- they will find the enthusiasm contagious.

Now, from the above, it must be perfectly clear that the most desirable camp to be in is the assertive group. Most of us, however, exhibit a mixture of different styles, and so to succeed in minimizing the negative effects of difficult behavioural patterns in others, it is necessary to move oneself as far as possible into the assertive area.

Who wins, after all?

Passive people rarely achieve their own goals because they seldom identify their own goals in the first place, relying on others to give them a lead.

Aggressive people often achieve their goals in the short term, but often this is at the expense of others and this fact can then backfire on them at a later date when they come face to face with antagonism and retaliation from those whom they have put down in the past. Worse still, there is no loyalty engendered in others during the process of 'winning', and so there is no pool of loyalty on which they can draw when times get tough.

It is assertive people who usually achieve their goals because in their view everyone can win. They are willing to negotiate for what is right rather than for short-term expediency, and they gain the respect of others while doing so.

 Enlightened self-awareness can enable us to get into the right attitude to make the most of our own assertiveness.

On Wednesday and Thursday we will see how putting ourselves into the balanced assertiveness camp can help us in handling conflict as well as with our basic communication skills.

Summary

Most styles of behaviour can be categorized as one of three basic types: passive, aggressive or assertive.

● Passive behaviour is most typified by people who put other people's needs before their own; they are often insecure and frustrated by their inability to be assertive, leading to feelings of inadequacy.

● Aggressive behaviour is typically satisfying one's own needs at the expense of others and being a bully. It often results from feelings of inadequacy and lack of self-worth, which does not allow the person to admit to faults.

● Assertive behaviour is a concern not only for one's own rights and opinions but also for those of others, and so the assertive person aims for a win–win situation.

In general, assertive people are the ones we most like to be associated with and, by moving towards the assertive area ourselves, we are better able to respond to passive and aggressive types.

SUNDAY
MONDAY
TUESDAY
WEDNESDAY
THURSDAY
FRIDAY
SATURDAY

Fact-check (answers at the back)

Some of these questions have more than one correct answer.

1. Which of the following are the main categories of behavioural style?
   a) Neutral ❏
   b) Passive ❏
   c) Aggressive ❏
   d) Assertive ❏

2. People who put other people's needs before their own often exhibit passive behaviour. What might this mean?
   a) They have little respect for themselves ❏
   b) They may be reluctant to stand up for themselves ❏
   c) They are very easy-going ❏
   d) They are often put upon by others ❏

3. What is a passive person likely to feel?
   a) Happy and confident ❏
   b) Angry and negative ❏
   c) Anxious and frustrated ❏
   d) Insecure and withdrawn ❏

4. What are those dealing with passive people are likely to feel?
   a) Energized and constructive ❏
   b) Annoyed and worn out ❏
   c) Supportive and enthusiastic ❏
   d) Withdrawn and negative ❏

5. People who satisfy their own needs at the expense of others often exhibit aggressive behaviour. What might this mean?
   a) They are often a verbal bully ❏
   b) They seem very confident ❏
   c) They lack self-worth ❏
   d) They get the best from others ❏

6. What are people who exhibit aggressive tendencies likely to feel?
   a) Guilty ❏
   b) Lonely ❏
   c) Powerful ❏
   d) None of the above ❏

7. What can people who exhibit aggressive behaviour cause others to feel?
   a) Motivated ❏
   b) Defensive ❏
   c) Humiliated ❏
   d) Withdrawn ❏

8. An assertive person is concerned not only for his own rights and opinions, but also for what?
   a) The rights and opinions of others ❏
   b) Achieving a win–win situation with others ❏
   c) Making compromises in a positive way ❏
   d) Not to be passionate in his arguments ❏

9. An assertive person often exhibits which of the following tendencies? ❏
a) An unfailing ability to alienate others ❏
b) Enthusiasm ❏
c) Good communication skills ❏
d) An understanding of other people's needs and feelings ❏

10. When dealing with assertive people, why are others likely to feel positive?
a) They know where they stand ❏
b) Even though they are not listened to, the end result will still be good ❏
c) They sense their success is a shared success ❏
d) They find the enthusiasm contagious ❏

TUESDAY

Coping with different problem people

The common trait exhibited by all problem people is that their behaviour causes problems for others. However, merely labelling them without attempting to understand them can be destructive, so if we want to change their behaviour so that we can work with them, we do need to try to understand their point of view.

Today we look at the four main categories of personality display: insecure, negative, selfish and pleasant. Each of these four types is explained and examples are given of likely behavioural displays, along with suggestions as to why the person may be acting in this manner. Advice is given on how to respond to each type, both in practical situations and in our own opinions of the other person.

Responding appropriately, and being able to approach an interaction in the correct frame of mind ourselves, has a very important effect on the outcome of individual interactions and therefore on the ongoing relationship. With some types, we may be able to achieve a more positive dialogue or response and with others we may even succeed in modifying the problem behaviour in the long term.

People problems

What do we mean by problem people? They come in all shapes and sizes, but the one common trait that they all exhibit is a type of behaviour that gives someone else a problem.

If you put your mind to it, you would probably be able to come up with at least 50 different types of behaviour that can cause problems for others. Being able to distinguish and categorize a particular type of behaviour will put you in a much better position to be able to do something about it. Of course, you could always ignore the problem, but that isn't very constructive and could even make the problem worse for others as well as for yourself. If you cannot even recognize what it is that someone does or says that causes problems for others, how are you going to be able to improve that person's behaviour for the future – or, more to the point, your reaction to it?

Not all people problems are necessarily daunting. Some types of behaviour might be a trifle irritating, but are easy enough to shrug off without needing to do anything further. Others, on the other hand, seem to have a never-ending impact and they can leave you feeling quite unable to work out how best to cope.

Very often, the person whose behaviour causes problems is totally unaware of the conflict he causes for others. That being the case, it works out that the person who has to deal with the problem is actually you. You have to 'own' the problem, just as if you were 'owning' a problem of late delivery or poor-quality production in a factory.

Yet, however inconsiderate or boorish someone else's behaviour, it is equally true that we all react to one another, and the way someone else reacts to you has a feedback effect on the way you behave in the first place. Sometimes we are therefore actually responsible for the problematic behaviour in others. While one could regard this as part and parcel of life's rich tapestry, it does matter, not least because:

● it creates unnecessary stress, leading to low morale
● it wastes time, because effort is being expended on griping instead of on productive work and relationships

- it distorts the decision-making process, since those who display difficult behaviour are often circumvented in order to ease the burden on others
- it can encourage a selective emigration of the best employees to more conducive working environments
- it stops work being in any way fun.

Dealing with problem people at work

When encountering a difficult person for the first time, it is all too easy to hate him or to label him as deficient in some way without properly understanding what he is going through. Yet if you are serious about wanting to change his behaviour, you will only be able to do so if you learn to understand him from his own point of view. Pigeonholing people on sight is one of the most destructive things you can do within a workplace or community.

Within a work environment, it might appear that those with behavioural problems can be broken down into three main categories:

1 Your supervisors
2 Your subordinates
3 Your fellow co-workers

The supervisors might be poor motivators, aggressive, or have poor supervisory skills; the subordinates might be error-prone, daydreamers, time wasters, or dishonest; while the co-workers might exhibit unprofessional behaviour such as putting things off, 'passing the buck', being overly critical or shirking.

While the way in which you might deal with the person will vary, depending on where they are in the hierarchical structure relative to you, each of these categories of worker can display common behavioural problems. So let's look at some of the more common types of behaviour and consider how we might deal with them.

Although there are very many types of personality display, we can break down the different behavioural patterns into four main categories:

1 **Insecure** – one of the most basic reasons for people displaying problematic behaviour
2 **Negative** – it can be very wearing to deal with this when exposed to such behaviour for long periods
3 **Selfish** – whether they are consciously so or oblivious to the fact that they are what they are, these types are easier to diagnose and to 'turn around'
4 **Pleasant** – this is sometimes the most difficult type of behaviour to deal with as you do not want to hurt their feelings.

Insecure people

Insecurity in people can take a number of forms. In its most basic, the insecure person needs to boost his own self-image, but the problem is that he does this by criticizing others. The eternal put-down can be very wearing, and if this then turns into your being hurt or even becoming openly hostile in return, it can have a bad effect on any kind of working relationship.

Perhaps worse still is the type who is, on the surface, perfectly pleasant to begin with, until something that most would regard as quite innocuous causes him to lose control and let fly with insults. Basically, this type of person has never quite got over the habit of his childhood tantrums and is turning on a defence mechanism; perhaps he feels personally threatened, or under pressure. His immediate response, therefore, is to react before anyone has even launched an attack on him.

Insecurity also makes itself felt by the ponderous types who either cannot make up their minds or always find some reason for putting off any kind of action. It may be that this kind of person has such low self-esteem that he is afraid that anything he does will be wrong, even though he genuinely wants to help. Equally, however, it may be that he simply does not feel that anyone else's efforts are good enough, and having asked someone to do something for him, he will then set about doing exactly the same task himself just to 'make sure' that the information, or whatever, is adequate. This can be taken to extremes by their forever trumpeting their triumphs and focusing everything on themselves rather than on the job in hand or other people.

On a bad day, dealing with insecure people can leave you wondering whether the effort is worthwhile. Yet all such responses need to attempt to build up that person's self-esteem by not knocking him down when he is – perhaps subconsciously – expecting that very reaction. Reassurance is all but, in addition, you should attempt:

● never to snap back, since this is what he may expect, and so by refraining from doing so you are breaking a vicious circle
● to be assertive in attempting to find out what the problem is from his point of view and to understand what is troubling him
● to remain absolutely silent if he is throwing a temper tantrum, and then ask him to explain himself
● to set deadlines for those normally incapable of setting timescales for themselves. This gives them confidence that it is not just their responsibility to meet deadlines.

You can also use humour to get you through difficult times with problem people. Conjuring up an amusing mental image of the difficult person can relieve the stress of having to be on the receiving end of some of his tirades. For instance, if your boss throws a temper tantrum, try picturing him still wearing a nappy and throwing his toys out of his pram. Such an image can do wonders to keep yourself calm while others around you are losing their cool.

Negative people

Negativity in a person is also very tiring to deal with and can be extremely depressing because if one is not careful it can almost infect you – in the same way that one person yawning in a room can often 'infect' others with the same action.

Such people may well be trying to protect themselves from future failure, but in so doing their immediate reaction is to ask 'What's the point?' Rarely will they come up with any better suggestions for carrying out a task. Worse, if you attempt to offer an alternative solution you are likely to get a similar negative response.

Another type of negative person is the aggressive, verbal bully – the type who believes he knows better than anyone else how something should be done and doesn't waste a moment in telling everyone of his infallibility. He will often tell you that you are wasting your time because you are not doing things his way. As often as not, he is very thorough and highly efficient, but his negative attitude towards others leads to feelings of resentment and means that people will then ignore him on principle.

The first thing when dealing with such people is not to let their negativity invade you. In addition, you could:

- try to get him to explain why he feels as he does
- tell him that as you are convinced in your own mind of the right course of action, you will take it anyway, regardless of whether he is 'with' you or not
- resist wasting time arguing with him
- ask yourself whether at the end of the day it is worth dealing with such a person anyway – assuming that's possible – since he is unlikely to change his behaviour and will continue to give you grief for some time to come!

 TIP *Make sure you have done your homework before tackling a negative, aggressive bully.*

Selfish people

Selfish people often act the way they do without pausing to consider for one moment that what they are doing is destructive or hurtful to others. Sometimes they are as they are because in childhood their parents had never trained them out of their natural selfish state that we are all born with. (Consider a baby crying, for instance. As far as he is concerned, his comforts are all that matters and, naturally, he has not yet learned that others have needs too.)

Very often, selfish people can be extremely irritating. If your next-door neighbour in a block of flats has his music system turned up too loud, he may well turn it down when asked to, but if he is basically selfish he will, as sure as anything, forget the next time around and have it up at full blast once again.

Selfish people will often be so busy telling others of their thoughts and needs that they may be oblivious to the fact that others might have something to say or an opinion to share. Those who bulldoze their way through life in this manner can be extremely disruptive in a work environment. Since they are so busy trying to get their own way, their co-workers may put up with this for a while but will soon start to build up resentment, which leads them to ostracize that person or, worse still, lose their temper with them. However, that is the last thing one should do since the selfish person will invariably win this type of 'argument'.

Another type of selfish behaviour is displayed by a fundamentally aggressive person who is covert in his attacks on others. The end result of this person's making jokes at others' expense, normally behind their backs, can be that the victim is much more hurt than he would be if the 'joke' had been made out in the open. If the victim then takes offence, the aggravator can accuse the victim of being a bad sport or of not being able to 'take a joke'.

This type of person thrives in front of an audience but will rarely continue such behaviour in private. So, to attempt to change his behaviour, you should:

- get him on his own, explain what he is doing and ask if he is genuinely trying to hurt you
- avoid getting into an argument with him, but do stand up to him and keep your body language assertive
- not sound either angry or submissive as this will feed his feelings of superiority
- if he is making derogatory remarks about you behind your back, suggest that in future he make them directly to you. He won't!

Pleasant people

Perhaps the most difficult people to deal with are those who are on the surface pleasant in their ways. This is because it makes us feel guilty to confront them with their problematic behaviour, especially if they react in a manner that shows that they are hurt that anyone could have found something wrong with them.

Not all pleasant, problematic people are wimps, of course. While some might keep a low profile because they are genuinely confused, others may be perfectly nice but just unreliable. Yet again, someone might be anxious to gain respect and friendship, but be unwilling to make any efforts to achieve this.

Some unreliable people need so much to feel liked by everyone that they will promise to do all kinds of things, and only subsequently realize that they cannot deliver their promises. They then feel obliged to make even more promises to make up for their earlier shortcomings, and a vicious circle sets in.

Although it can be embarrassing to deal with such people, they are probably the most worthwhile in the end to have to deal with since there is a good chance that you can turn them around to face the realities of a situation and they can then become valued players in a team. The trick here is to offer reassurance that they are likeable and that their views are valued, just so long as they are willing to say what they think, rather than agree with everyone simply to keep the peace. In addition, you should:

● keep your body language open and friendly
● reassure them that you value their opinions
● pay them compliments, so long as these are genuine, in order to demonstrate that they really are valued members of the team
● encourage them to come up with suggestions and solutions to problems
● help them save face by stating the facts, rather than your opinions, and then getting them to suggest ideas of their own.

We said at the beginning of this chapter that it should be easy enough to think of at least 50 different types of problematic behaviour. The four main categories that we have just looked at will not necessarily encompass every one, just as many problem people will exhibit characteristics of more than one of them. But by reaching out and attempting to understand what it is that drives someone to behave in the way that he does, you will have a better chance of being able to turn him around from being a difficult person to a valued member of your team.

Summary

The best way to change the behaviour of difficult people is to see how the world looks through their eyes. It is useful to categorize different behavioural patterns as one of four main types: insecure, negative, selfish and pleasant.

● Insecure people essentially lack confidence, so they criticize others or are indecisive. All responses need to attempt to build up that person's self-esteem.

● Negative people may well be trying to protect themselves from future failure by asking, 'What's the point?' or insisting that their way is the correct way. It is important not to let the negativity be infectious or to waste time arguing.

● Selfish people often act without considering that what they are doing may be destructive or harmful to others, so it is useful to keep calm and explain it to them.

● Those who are pleasant may be easier to cope with as they can be helped to face the realities of a situation, having been reassured that they are likeable and valuable.

SUNDAY
MONDAY
TUESDAY
WEDNESDAY
THURSDAY
FRIDAY
SATURDAY

Fact-check (answers at the back)

Some of these questions have more than one correct answer.

1. Which of the following problems does difficult behaviour cause, if it is left unchecked?
a) Unnecessary stress, leading to low morale ☐
b) Time wasting, because effort is spent on confrontation instead of work ☐
c) It distorts the decision-making process ☐
d) None of the above, if the difficult behaviour is ignored ☐

2. Although there are many types of personality display, the different behavioural patterns may be divided into how many categories?
a) Two ☐
b) Four ☐
c) Six ☐
d) Eight ☐

3. Insecurity in people can take a number of forms. Which of the following traits are attributable?
a) Frequently criticizing others ☐
b) Never venturing an opinion ☐
c) Being unable to make up one's mind ☐
d) Trumpeting one's own triumphs ☐

4. In dealing with insecure people, what do we need to do?
a) Avoid 'snapping' at them ☐
b) Set deadlines for those normally incapable of setting their own timescales ☐
c) Not ask them to do anything which they may find challenging ☐
d) Remain silent during a temper tantrum and afterwards ask them to explain themselves ☐

5. Which of the following traits may be attributed to negative people?
a) 'Infecting' and depressing others with their mindset ☐
b) Asking 'What's the point?' ☐
c) Telling others they are wasting their time ☐
d) Saying that their own way does not work ☐

6. Which of the following methods may be successful in dealing with a negative person?
a) Spending time arguing with them ☐
b) Not preparing before a conversation so your responses are spontaneous ☐
c) Telling him you are going to proceed with your plans anyway, despite his reservations ☐
d) Trying to get him to explain why he feels as he does ☐

7. Which of the following statements apply to selfish people?
a) They act without consideration for others ❑
b) They frequently tell others of their own thoughts and needs ❑
c) They work well in a team ❑
d) Their method of bulldozing through is effective in a work environment ❑

8. To change the behaviour of a selfish person, what should you do?
a) Treat him as he treats others ❑
b) Sound angry, to put him in his place ❑
c) In private, explain to him the effect of his actions ❑
d) Avoid getting into an argument with him, but stand up to him ❑

9. Of the following, what makes difficult people who are pleasant on the surface a challenge to deal with?
a) There is no such thing as a difficult person who is pleasant ❑
b) It makes us feel guilty to confront them with their problematic behaviour ❑
c) They may promise things they are unable to deliver ❑
d) They might be anxious to gain respect and friendship but unwilling to make an effort to achieve this ❑

10. In order to make pleasant but difficult people valuable members of the team, what should you do?
a) Reassure them that you value their opinions ❑
b) Only give them tasks in which they cannot fail ❑
c) Encourage them to come up with suggestions and solutions to problems ❑
d) Constantly monitor them so failure to deliver is not an option ❑

WEDNESDAY

Managing conflict situations

Today we look at how to manage conflict situations, which are an inevitable part of life. It is how we manage this conflict that is so important: to achieve compromise, to maintain a logical response and not to be ruled by our emotions, so that the conflict does not become negative.

Through observing the way in which conflict is handled, four different personality types may be determined: dictatorial, enthusiastic, empathetic and processor. The manner in which these personality types handle conflict is different, influencing both their experience of the process and its likely outcome. We'll look at examples of likely behaviours of each type and suggestions for appropriate responses. A successful outcome will require different approaches, according to the style of the person with whom we are in conflict.

There is a specific focus on handling conflict with clients, revealing the five main reasons why a customer might become annoyed with a company. You will learn how to make a competent response to complaints, whether the interaction is face to face, by phone, by email or social networking, with each form of communication requiring a particular etiquette.

The causes of conflicts

Conflicts invariably stem from one root cause: in essence both sides want to have their own way, and unless a compromise is achieved, conflict is inevitable. Throughout our lives, we have to come to terms with the conflicting forces of logic and emotion. Sometimes it is all too easy to react emotionally, but inevitably it is when our reactions are based on logic that we are better able to handle difficult circumstances. We must also not forget that the emotional content of our relationships gives them their raison d'être and comfort zones – as well as the potential for conflict. Emotion must be valued too.

To many people, it is much more difficult to get into gear with a logical approach, but it is, nonetheless, perfectly possible to develop the ability to use logic by first analysing a situation and then applying techniques to control your feelings and reactions instead of allowing your emotions to rule the day. It is really a question of saying to yourself:

- Let's step back and look at the situation a bit more clearly.
- Let's get the emotion out of this.
- How can we move this situation forward towards achieving the common objectives?

Only then can individual problems and sensitivities be accommodated rather than their dominating and waylaying progress within the relationships.

There are, of course, many reasons for conflict between two parties. For instance:

- each may wish to achieve different goals
- there is a difference in perception of the problems involved
- there is a clash of personalities, which stifles communication
- each party may be in competition with the other
- either party might not want the responsibility imposed by a certain course of action
- there is poor communication.

Although such conflict can cause depression or apathy, it is equally true that many stressful situations can lead to positive results, such as the generation of enthusiasm or the finding of a solution to a problem that had remained stubbornly impenetrable. So the problem is not actually a situation where there is conflict, but more one where the conflict is negative – where stress turns itself into distress.

The real danger of stressful conflict is that it can be so damaging. For instance:

- it can divert attention away from the real issues behind the conflict, and the objectives can be lost
- one or both parties to the conflict can become so frustrated that it impedes a settlement, and ultimately one or both sides become uncooperative.

Many conflict situations arise because one of the parties feels that someone is attempting to take advantage of him, or because he feels he has to defend himself against an aggressive person. Basically, when any conflict situation arises there are three possible outcomes:

1 Both sides can pretend there is really no problem. If the matter is not particularly important, then this can often be the best outcome.
2 One person wins, while the other loses. This may solve the present conflict, but it can cause an imbalance that can lead to a build-up of resentment and make it more difficult to resolve the next crisis point.

3 Each person understands that the final solution has to take account of both parties' wishes. By working to a common goal, both sides have to make compromises, but the final solution is stronger because of this.

In understanding what situations lead to conflict, a person will more easily be able to avoid it. There are, of course, no hard and fast rules about reducing potential conflicts, but the following list demonstrates some of the areas that are ripe for examination:

● By attempting to see things from other people's points of view, you are better able to accept that no one person is ever always right or wrong.
● It is equally not possible for everyone always to agree on everything. By accepting the fact that compromise is better than conflict, you are better able to find a way forward rather than wallowing in an impasse.
● Many of us are all too prone to make snap judgements. It follows from the above that if we can hear out the other person without jumping to conclusions, we will be better able to find a way forward.

When it comes to recognizing the early stages of a conflict in the making, very often the cause has more to do with the characters involved than the situation itself. If logic is the most positive way of resolving a conflict, it follows that wherever emotion gets a stranglehold, a resolution can become more difficult.

Conflict and personality types

When it comes to handling conflict, determining different personality types can be useful. Most people can be diagnosed as being in one of four basic categories: dictatorial, enthusiastic, empathetic or processor.

Dictators

Perhaps the most difficult type of personality to come to terms with, dictatorial people tend to be egoists in the extreme. They always want to have their own way and will often bulldoze people into submission. Often they can be extremely hurtful because they say what they think regardless of how others will react. They are totally results-oriented and have little time for individuals.

The problem in dealing with such people is that being aggressive in return is generally counter-productive. Similarly, acting submissively will only reinforce their feelings of superiority. The only sure way of interacting with a dictator is to deal in facts, for to them, facts are an extension of logic. This will also enable you to get to the heart of the matter at the earliest opportunity, and to reach a solution. They may well have alienated you in the process, but ultimately that will be their problem. The main thing to ensure is that it should not be yours!

Enthusiasts

Enthusiasts are normally energetic and have a strong ability to motivate others. They can often be described as charismatic and are often popular. Enthusiasts are sometimes wont to talk rapidly and loudly, but ultimately if they do not get the necessary feedback they are more likely to drop out of a project before seeing it through to completion.

Dealing with enthusiasts requires you to be almost as energetic as they are. Offering support and encouragement is the most likely way to get the best out of them and to work with them – and to get any project happily completed.

Empathizers

Into this camp fall what are sometimes referred to as 'people persons'. They are typically genuinely caring but are not the best at getting things done in a hurry, and can be frustratingly indecisive.

Accordingly, if you want to get the best from an empathizer it is wise not to hurry him, and to listen attentively to what he has to say.

Processors

Such people, who may appear somewhat tedious or boring on the outside, nevertheless exhibit analytical skills that involve paying great attention to detail. They are usually efficient, if a little on the unimaginative side, and organized in the extreme. Processor types often end up in professions such as accountancy where accuracy and detail are paramount; but it is not for nothing that comedians tend to use them for the butt of their jokes (e.g. Monty Python's 'Ich bin ein Chartered Accountant' sketch).

Dealing with processor types invariably works well when presenting them with logic and facts. They are not always the fastest thinkers, as they like to assimilate new information, building on and assessing it with what they already know. In addition, they invariably lack vision and, as a result, take longer to buy in to a new concept.

TIP *Although not everyone falls precisely into one category or another, it is useful to be aware, when taking these four basic types, that conflict can easily arise if, for instance, a processor comes into discussion with a dictatorial person or an enthusiast has to deal with an empathizer.*

Conflict with clients and customers

Just as it can be exasperating to deal with difficult colleagues at work, it is often even more problematic dealing with difficult clients or customers. The old axiom that 'the client is always right' may well form the backbone of customer service, but it can leave employees feeling frustrated and stressed.

Those at the receiving end of a customer's anger – be it at the end of a phone, in a meeting face to face, or by electronic communication – are often the main point of contact between a client and a company, and so they become the butt of the client's anger. Yet, reacting in an impatient or insensitive manner is not the way to get the customer to move over to your point of view, and certainly not the stuff of professional customer relationships and service.

Nowadays, especially, where customer service is what differentiates one company from another in an increasingly global marketplace, any form of negative behaviour or reaction from a company employee could result in a customer staying away and taking his business elsewhere, which is considerably easier since the arrival of the Internet. Worse still, he may tell his friends and they could stay away too. Trying to win a customer back is twice as difficult as landing him in the first place – as if that wasn't hard enough! So the way in which an employee acts with, and reacts to, a customer can be far more important than the advertising or PR that a company puts together to build up its image.

Successfully dealing with difficult clients necessitates putting yourself in the client's shoes and understanding what it is that makes him annoyed or, even more basically, what he wanted in the first place. There are at least two sides from which to look at every situation, and people don't generally complain unless they have something specific to 'beef' about.

By finding out what it is that the client is unhappy about, you can then concentrate on solving his problem. Remember, he is not necessarily interested in a third party finding a solution. As far as he is concerned, you are the company representative and so it is up to you to find a solution. Your blaming another part of the organization will only inflame the situation further.

Why a customer may be difficult

In general, a customer can get annoyed with a company for one of five main reasons:

1 He feels no one will listen to him.
2 Something went wrong, and he feels no one is willing to accept responsibility or give redress.
3 He needs help or guidance, but can find no one to give it to him.
4 The product does not work or the service provided is inadequate.
5 He thought through and planned everything to do with the purchase or installation, and yet it still went wrong.

It may not, of course, be possible for you to be the solution provider. So what should you do? The first thing is to attempt to find a position of empathy with his plight. Nothing is more frustrating than feeling that no one understands your problem. So, by showing understanding and getting over to his side, you are immediately getting rid of his first frustration. Only then should you start to help deal with the problem.

Sometimes, customers are not really sure what they do want, apart from tearing someone off a strip for the wrongs they feel they have suffered. So a good technique is, having empathized with their situation, to ask what they would like you to do to help out. It may well be that you personally can't help him in this case; so state what you can do, offering one or two alternatives. You have effectively returned control of the situation to the customer. Sometimes there will be nothing at all you can do – in which case you will need to explain the company's policies and try to find with him a common solution.

TIP *By spending time showing sympathy and understanding, you might not have put things totally to rights, but your client will know that he is not likely to get the brush-off – which is what angers people the most.*

Dealing with someone face to face is often easier than doing so over the telephone or by email because you can use body language to convey your feelings. However, there are some standard guidelines for dealing with difficult clients over the phone:

- Always follow the '3 Ps' code: come across as professional, polite and pleasant.
- Make the caller feel important.
- Try to avoid wasting not just the caller's time but the company's time as well.
- Help the caller achieve his desired objectives.

Email has its own guidelines:

- Address the customer with respect.
- Deal with the problems succinctly.
- Be aware that the immediate nature of the medium can exacerbate misunderstandings.
- Ensure you build a personal relationship rather than remain anonymous.

Whether the conflict situation is over the email or phone, face to face or on Skype, you should always remain cool and calm and do your best to appear concerned but impartial at all times. There is nothing wrong with expressing contradictory ideas, but the secret is in knowing how to put them across without it escalating into a heated debate.

At the end of the day, it is not the fact that you have a contradictory idea that causes problems; more, it is the fact that two personality traits come into opposition. The first should not be smothered; the latter should be circumvented if at all possible.

Summary

Conflict does not always have to be stressful. Indeed, if used constructively, conflict may lead to positive results such as solving a problem. Stressful conflict can be damaging if it diverts attention away from the real issues and if it upsets one or both parties because they feel taken advantage of or treated aggressively. Sometimes it may be possible to avoid conflict by understanding and avoiding the situations that lead to it.

To resolve a conflict, it may be helpful to appreciate that the cause often has more to do with the people than with the situation itself, so we need to handle appropriately the different personality types involved. Deal in facts with dictator and processor types; be energetic, supportive and encouraging with an enthusiastic person; be patient with and listen attentively to an empathizer. Dealing successfully with difficult clients requires an understanding of what it was they wanted in the first place so that you can meet their needs if possible, or at least attempt to find a position of empathy.

SUNDAY
MONDAY
TUESDAY
WEDNESDAY
THURSDAY
FRIDAY
SATURDAY

Fact-check (answers at the back)

Some of these questions have more than one correct answer.

1. Conflicts invariably stem from one root cause, which is what?
   a) People rarely work well in teams ❏
   b) People are always competitive ❏
   c) Both sides want to have their own way ❏
   d) Pride ❏

2. In a conflict situation, how should we deal with the conflicting forces of logic and emotion?
   a) We should always react emotionally ❏
   b) Emotions have no place or value ❏
   c) Emotions need to be kept under control, as it is when our reactions are based on logic that we fare better in difficult circumstances ❏
   d) In a difficult situation, an emotional response can be the right one ❏

3. What are the dangers of stressful conflict?
   a) All potential for a positive resolution is lost ❏
   b) It can divert attention from the real issues ❏
   c) Enthusiasm and problem solving become impossible ❏
   d) The frustration of one or both parties may impede a settlement ❏

4. In a conflict situation, there is more than one possible outcome. Which is the best solution?
   a) Both sides walking away, refusing to fight ❏
   b) Both sides pretending there is no problem ❏
   c) One person wins, while the other loses ❏
   d) Each person understanding that the final solution has to take account of both parties' wishes ❏

5. How many different personality types are there with regard to handling conflict?
   a) Two ❏
   b) Three ❏
   c) Four ❏
   d) Five ❏

6. Which of the following statements are true for interactions with dictator personalities?
   a) They will always want to have their own way ❏
   b) They say what they think without regard for others ❏
   c) Being aggressive in return is generally counterproductive ❏
   d) The only way to work with them is by acting submissively ❏

7. Which of the following statements are true for interactions with enthusiastic personalities?
a) They are normally energetic ❏
b) They have a strong ability to motivate others ❏
c) Offering support and encouragement causes enthusiastic types to get carried away and fail at the task ❏
d) They are inclined to talk rapidly and loudly ❏

8. Which of the following statements are true for interactions with empathizers?
a) They are not the best at getting things done ❏
b) They need to be hurried along ❏
c) They can be frustratingly indecisive ❏
d) They are typically genuinely caring ❏

9. Which of the following statements are true for interactions with processors?
a) They are quick to grasp new concepts with few facts required ❏
b) Their analytical skills are strong ❏
c) They pay attention to detail ❏
d) They often lack vision ❏

10. Successfully dealing with difficult clients necessitates what?
a) Understanding what they want in the first place ❏
b) Responding to them in a like-for-like manner; if they shout, you shout ❏
c) Blaming another part of the company to defuse their anger with you ❏
d) Empathizing with the situation and asking what they see as a resolution ❏

SUNDAY

MONDAY

TUESDAY

WEDNESDAY

THURSDAY

FRIDAY

SATURDAY

THURSDAY

Basic communication skills and body language

You have now been introduced to several helpful methods for dealing with difficult people. We need to understand ourselves, identify types of behaviour, recognize behavioural patterns and manage conflict situations. Influencing and informing all these concepts are our basic communication skills and body language.

Today you will learn why good communication is more than just speaking and listening, but also requires comprehension. We are reminded that while we may consider ourselves to be coherent, it is still possible for us to be misunderstood and suggestions are given for facilitating good communication.

The relevance of non-verbal signals is also highlighted, as these signals may either reinforce what we are saying or cast doubt on its validity, depending on our physical mannerisms. Equally, we may be able to use the body language of the person with whom we are interacting to assess the honesty of what they are saying or how comfortable they feel with the discussion. Examples of non-verbal signals are given, with explanations of what these might signify. Actions may be both voluntary and involuntary and by learning to read the signs you will be better placed to control the situation.

Problems of communication

Communication is at the heart of any relationship between two people; and very often a lack of good communication is the single most important barrier to getting on with a so-called 'difficult person'.

Anyone who feels he is consistently misunderstood is often guilty of nothing more than his own propensity to make assumptions. What you think you say and what someone else understands you to say are very often not the same. The lack of care in writing emails often exacerbates the problem. Reread them before you send them off!

For instance, you might *think* you say something, but *actually* say something else. Someone else might *think* you said something but *actually* hear something else. He might then *think* he has responded to you in a certain way, but *actually* responded differently, and you might *think* he has responded in a certain way even though you *actually* heard him say something else. Confused? So you should be. It was all wrapped up rather nicely when Humpty Dumpty said, 'Words mean what you want them to mean.'

Even though a speaker may actually be perfectly coherent, he may still be misunderstood. This is often as much to do with the listener as the speaker. Consider, for instance, whether the listener:

- has a low level of concentration – he may not actually be taking in what you are saying
- is prejudiced in some way – in which case he will automatically be colouring the meaning of what you are saying
- has a headache – he is more likely to be distracted from listening attentively
- has no background experience of what you are saying – in which case, how will he assimilate new material when there is no 'peg' in his mind on which to hang it?
- is stressed in some way and so unlikely to be able to concentrate
- feels out of his depth in the subject matter and therefore expects not to understand.

There are numerous other reasons why someone might not take on board all your instructions. Often, the use of paraphrasing what you are saying is a good way around this problem as what it does is to reach the listener from a number of different viewpoints, thereby offering a better chance for the message to get through. It also shows that the message is getting through in the way that the speaker intended. In this way misunderstandings can be avoided – and that has to be a good thing in any communication situation.

Improving communication

Feedback is another important part of the communication process. This can not only show how you react to something someone is saying, but can also help the speaker clarify his message if this is not getting through. The best salespeople always ensure they have the necessary feedback – and a lot can be learned from them.

To amplify, it is entirely appropriate to offer feedback in order to let others know when:

- you have understood what they are saying
- you have not understood what they are saying
- you are upset or embarrassed about what they have said
- you disagree with what they are saying
- you approve of what they are saying
- you are amused by what they have said.

Gossip plays an essential part in communication processes. It can reinforce the interest, understanding and comfort we find in one another and thereby put us on a common plain when communicating with others. A little social intercourse can often identify potential problems before they turn into a conflict.

 TIP *So that there are no misunderstandings in email, writing your reply in a different colour throughout the received email can ensure that each point is dealt with, thereby more easily diffusing a difficult situation.*

In giving feedback, you should:

- make sure the speaker is ready to receive your contra-messages
- be specific, rather than giving 'woolly' examples

- do so as soon as possible after the event so that the subject is still 'warm' in the speaker's mind
- do so in private if at all possible, if it is a sensitive situation, since it can be quite damaging if done in front of others
- be positive in order to lead the situation forward
- encourage the recipient to give feedback in a like manner so that no one is seen to be scoring points at the other's expense.

Of course, some people are much more difficult to deal with than others, and there is always a danger, when giving feedback to a difficult person, that your attempt could backfire, especially if he is higher up than you in the management hierarchy. In such cases, advance preparation is absolutely essential.

Preparing to give feedback

1 Begin by identifying the problem and concentrating on what can be improved by the person in question.

2 If possible, try to determine why the person is behaving in such a manner.

3 Be prepared for a confrontation if giving a difficult person feedback about his general or specific behaviour. How will you handle his reactions? Try to imagine what defence he will come up with.

4 Rehearse both your arguments and counter-reactions thoroughly so that you know instinctively what you are going to do or say at the right time.

5 Be positive in what you say to the difficult person. Explain simply why what he does or says upsets you, and express your willingness to help him adapt his ways.

6 Try to work out and agree a plan of action on both his and your part.

7 Comment positively on progress that you observe in his behaviour in order to encourage him further.

Body language and communication

Luckily, good communication is not just about speaking and listening. Although they are obviously very important, the words account for only a small proportion of any useful amount of comprehension between two people. The intonation and expressions inherent in the voice are also key factors, as are the messages contained in what we call 'body language'. Since speaking and listening are only two parts of any communication process, being able to interpret non-verbal signals in face-to-face meetings is therefore an extremely important adjunct in ensuring understanding.

All of us have a propensity to 'hear' other people by observing their physical reactions. Indeed, it is said that you can sometimes tell much more from watching someone than from listening to what they are saying. Usually this feedback is positive in that it reinforces what someone is saying, at the same time demonstrating what we feel inside. But equally, body language can give false signals that can override the verbal message being given out, and thereby harm the communication process.

There are very many types of body language, just a few of which are listed below. What do you read into the situation when you see someone:

- frowning? Usually this indicates that he either disagrees with what is being said or simply doesn't understand.
- avoiding eye contact? This is a sure sign that he is bored or lacks confidence, or perhaps he has something to hide.
- scratching his nose? He may be puzzled or may dislike something, but equally he may just have an itchy nose!
- speaking rapidly? Perhaps he is anxious or worried.
- raising his voice? It is likely that he is angry or worried.
- shifting from one foot to the other? He might be impatient, but equally he might have been standing for too long!

People who lie often give themselves away by their body language, while those who are genuine are usually easy to spot. Liars will often avoid looking directly at you while blinking or swallowing rapidly, clearing the throat or covering their mouths while speaking.

It is not for nothing that the expression 'having a poker face' is used to convey the picture of someone who has so mastered the control of his involuntary body movements that it is well nigh impossible to guess what he is thinking. But would you trust someone with a poker face? Whatever it was that he said, the chances are that you would instinctively mistrust him.

Variations in the amount of eye contact can also tell you a great deal about the person with whom you are conversing. Think back to when you were last angry with someone. Did you look him right in the eye as you spoke to him? As a rule of thumb, most people are comfortable with eye contact for up to around five seconds. Anything more than that and it can make the recipient feel uncomfortable – which is exactly why aggressive people stare out those whom they feel to be their inferiors.

Fixing someone with a stare is not the same action, of course, that two people in love appear to enjoy. If you look at the latter, their eyes dart backwards and forwards between the eyes and across the face – very different from a single fixed stare.

When people blink a lot, this can also be a sign that they are nervous, which itself may be an indication that they are not being entirely truthful with you – but they might also be contact-lens wearers and therefore need to blink a lot! On the other hand, if someone hardly blinks at all, this could indicate that they are either listening intently to what you are saying or watching for your reactions. As always, there is no hard and fast rule about what to look out for, but rather it is a combination of different signs.

Understanding personality types through body language

Summing up, what should we look out for when trying to interpret someone's body language? Getting back to our three types of behaviour – aggressive, passive and assertive – there are certain behavioural patterns that become all too obvious if you know what to look for.

For instance, someone who is assertive will usually maintain good eye contact, be relaxed and will smile or nod to encourage the other person as he speaks. A submissive person, on the other hand, will often lower his eyes in a downcast position so as to avoid eye contact; he might have a poor posture such as slouching or drooping his shoulders, and he might cover his mouth with his hand in a defensive attitude. Someone who is aggressive, however, will often maintain unwavering eye contact while standing with his feet apart and placing his hands on his hips in an impatient or irritated manner.

These same three behavioural types can also be identified from such a simple thing as shaking hands. For instance, an aggressor will often tend to grasp your hand firmly with his own uppermost and his palm facing downwards. A passive person will offer his palm face up, while the assertive type will tend to shake your hand at the same angle as yours – i.e. at right angles to the floor.

But you can take it even further than this. How often have you been to a party and experienced all manner of handshakes?

- There's the traditional limp shake whereby a floppy hand suggests that here is a weak and indecisive person.
- Someone who grasps your hand tightly may well be the type of person who wants to show he is both tough and in complete control.
- People who proffer just their fingers and thumb rather than their whole hand are as often as not insecure.
- Someone who holds his arm out stiffly might covertly be suggesting to you that he intends to be in control of the entire situation.

However, you still have to bear in mind any physical disabilities in this too. The person who does not notice arthritis in a hand that he has to shake may cause anxiety and pain when shaking hands firmly instead of the friendly gesture that was intended.

Non-verbal language can therefore be very useful in summing up a particular type of person. Body language often reflects a person's mental approach to life, and difficult people, in particular, will often give themselves away by their actions – both voluntary and involuntary.

By learning to read non-verbal signals, you will be in a much better position to adjust your own responses and to be in more control of a difficult situation.

Summary

Good communication skills are essential to any relationship, including that with a so-called 'difficult person'. Since it is as easy to misunderstand another as to be misunderstood ourselves, it is always good practice to speak clearly and listen well to avoid misunderstandings.

Another important tool in good communication is to give feedback; this not only shows your reactions to what you are hearing but can also help the speaker clarify their message if this is not getting through. Paraphrasing what has been said can also be useful, as alternative words may clarify any ambiguities. When giving feedback to a difficult person, advance preparation is essential to enable us to anticipate and appropriately deal with their response.

Speaking and listening, however, are only two of our communication skills; non-verbal signals can also be very useful. Our body language may reinforce or undermine what we are saying, or reveal thoughts even if they are unspoken.

SUNDAY

MONDAY

TUESDAY

WEDNESDAY

THURSDAY

FRIDAY

SATURDAY

Fact-check (answers at the back)

Some of these questions have more than one correct answer.

1. Which of the following statements apply to good communication?
a) It relies solely on speaking and listening ❏
b) It entails use of intonation and expression in the voice ❏
c) It is aided by 'body language' ❏
d) Misunderstanding never arises when communication is good ❏

2. Why is feedback an important part of the communication process?
a) It allows the listener to interrupt the speaker ❏
b) It lets others know you have understood what they are saying ❏
c) It lets others know you have not understood what they are saying ❏
d) It lets others know you are upset or embarrassed about what they have said ❏

3. In giving feedback, what should you do?
a) Try to catch the speaker off guard ❏
b) Not worry about being specific; vague feedback is sufficient ❏
c) Do so as soon as possible after the event ❏
d) Be positive ❏

4. Advance preparation is essential when giving feedback to a difficult person. Which of the following may prove helpful?
a) Having an aggressive stance from the beginning so the listener knows you mean what you say ❏
b) Trying to determine why the person is behaving in such a manner ❏
c) Making it up as you go along, so it seems natural ❏
d) Being prepared for confrontation, so you can handle his reactions ❏

5. It is said you can sometimes tell much more from watching someone than from listening to what they are saying. Which of the following statements are correct?
a) Non-verbal signals are always honest ❏
b) Non-verbal signals are always reliable ❏
c) What appears to be a non-verbal signal may be an indicator of some physical discomfort ❏
d) Non-verbal signals can be helpful in reinforcing or hinting at a meaning ❏

6. Eye contact is a very important part of communication. Which of the following statements apply?

a) Variations in the amount of eye contact can tell you a great deal about the person with whom you are conversing ❑

b) Liars will often avoid looking directly at you ❑

c) Aggressive people 'stare out' those whom they feel to be inferior ❑

d) A person who is unable to make eye contact with you cannot be trusted ❑

7. Which of the following is likely to be body language displayed by an assertive person?

a) Maintenance of good eye contact ❑

b) A relaxed stance ❑

c) A formality in approach ❑

d) Smiling and nodding to encourage the person speaking ❑

8. Which of the following is likely to be body language displayed by a passive personality?

a) Avoiding eye contact ❑

b) Standing too close to the speaker and invading their personal space ❑

c) Poor posture ❑

d) Covering his mouth with his hand in a defensive posture ❑

9. Which of the following is likely to be body language displayed by a person behaving aggressively? ❑

a) Listening carefully, with the head to one side to show you have their attention ❑

b) Maintaining unwavering eye contact ❑

c) Standing with hands on hips in an impatient manner ❑

d) Handshaking with his own hand uppermost ❑

10. Is it possible to learn anything about personality type from a handshake?

a) No – it's just a mannerism and doesn't reveal anything ❑

b) Sometimes, but you need to be careful that there is not an underlying physical cause for the mannerism ❑

c) Yes – it could be that someone who grasps your hand tightly may well want to show that they are tough and in control ❑

d) Yes – it could be that someone who proffers just their fingers and thumb rather than their whole hand may be insecure ❑

SUNDAY

MONDAY

TUESDAY

WEDNESDAY

THURSDAY

FRIDAY

SATURDAY

FRIDAY

How to say no and deal with difficult clients

Saying no is something the vast majority of us find very difficult to do. We like to be helpful, we want others to like us and we certainly don't want to appear selfish or uncaring. However, there are occasions when an honest 'No' is the correct response. Today we will consider the instances when we might find it difficult to say no, and the negative feelings we may experience following our failure to pluck up the courage to say it. Worse still, we might cause a difficult situation through our failure to say no and thereby risk becoming a difficult person ourselves!

Today we will look at some positive, constructive ways of saying no that will prevent us from feeling as though we are being obstructive and that will avoid giving offence. You will learn why saying no in certain situations may be more helpful than we might at first imagine. Saying no to a client brings further challenges and we will consider this scenario in detail, highlighting when it is appropriate to say no and how to handle this eventuality with courtesy, whether on the phone or in person.

The consequences of not saying no

Most people find it difficult to say no. It is in our nature not to do so for a number of reasons, not least because we want to avoid confrontation and we all feel the need to be liked and to be appreciated, and refusing a request can risk making us appear selfish to others.

The problem is that, by not being able to say what we really feel on such occasions, there is not just a possibility but a distinct likelihood that we will become over-burdened, and this can lead to stress and worry. This is particularly true in the workplace where, by agreeing to do everything that is asked of you, you could end up with an in-tray a mile high, while others appear to cope much more easily.

Nobody likes to feel taken advantage of, yet a person who has difficulty saying no is the very type to feel put upon by his work colleagues. If he refuses to do what is asked of him, he may well feel that he will no longer be liked or appreciated by the person doing the asking. He might even be fearful of an aggressive reaction if he says no to the request and therefore caves in since he may feel it is the better of the two options to cope with.

The point is, though, that if you were really too busy to take on some extra work, no one will thank you for handing in something that has been rushed and is of low quality. By avoiding causing displeasure in the first place by not refusing to take something on, you are much more likely to compound the problem at a later date. Such a scenario is especially true where a boss hands a subordinate vast amounts of work, knowing that that person is normally efficient and trustworthy.

TIP *By failing to make a stand at work when you think you have been asked to take on too much, you are likely to store up problems for the future.*

Why it's hard to say no

You might be unwilling to say no to your boss or colleagues for any of the following reasons:

- You don't wish to appear inefficient or incapable of completing the task.

- You're afraid that your boss will get angry and that ultimately this could put your job 'on the line'.

- You want to be liked and appreciated by all your colleagues.

- You want to improve your prospects for promotion.

- You have low self-esteem and want to build up the esteem of others.

However, you are much more likely to be appreciated by others if you are open and honest with your work colleagues, rather than struggling on alone, trying to keep up and ultimately not producing work of the required standard. It is quite possible, for instance, that the person asking you to do something might not have appreciated how much you already have on your plate; and how can he plan his own workload properly if he gets no feedback from you on whether what he is asking is reasonable or not?

By struggling on and then not managing to cope, you are much more likely to cause others to get angry with you – so the whole point of caving in to the original request backfires dramatically. So by not saying no, you can easily shoot yourself in the foot and become inefficient and late in your work – and ultimately overtired and unable to cope at all.

Now think of it the other way around. By being assertive and explaining that you cannot take on yet another piece of work, you are more likely to gain the respect of others and also to allow them to understand that there is a physical limitation that everyone comes up against in being able to cope with all that is thrown at them.

There is also the question of self-respect. Those who fail to produce quality work – regardless of whether it is 'their fault' or not – often end up with a low estimation of themselves. If, on top of that, they realize that by having the courage to stand up for themselves they could have avoided the situation in the first place, they are likely to feel doubly dejected.

Of course, if others perceive you to be someone who has little self-respect, they will begin to start treating you in that way, and any negative feelings towards you could intensify. At the opposite end of the scale, if others see you as being a positive person, then that is how they will react to you.

The problem that many find extremely difficult is just how to say no – especially to a superior member of staff. Doing so by making excuses is definitely not the way to do it. Apart from the fact that these excuses can either sound very lame or be seen for what they are – telling outright lies – they are also highly likely to make the apologist feel nothing short of cowardly, which again is hardly likely to make him feel good about himself.

How to say no to a colleague

The only way you can say no in this context is to be assertive. That does not mean that you have to be aggressive in your response; but by explaining why you cannot or will not do something someone has asked you to do, you may well find that it actually clears the air rather than making the situation more difficult.

Of course, you will want to have convinced yourself first of all that what is being requested of you is something that you cannot or do not want to do. It may even be that you will need to ask for further details before you make up your mind. But it is much better to refuse at the outset once your mind is made up, rather than let it fester in the background.

It often helps to give a good reason why you do not wish to carry out a particular request. This does not mean that you should hand out a string of excuses. The person whose request you are refusing will respect you much more if you quietly, but firmly, explain your reasons for refusal, keeping your emotions firmly under control.

Finally, if you really do want to help the other person but are unable to do so for whatever reason, it can do no harm to ask him if there is any way you can help him to find another solution to his problem.

Dealing with a difficult client

Saying no to one's boss or work colleagues is one thing. Saying no to a customer or client is quite a different matter. Being on the front line, representing the company, can often be quite a stressful experience. We all know the expression 'The customer is always right', but in reality it can be quite galling having to deal with difficult clients.

We are all clients or customers, and we all appreciate being shown courtesy and consideration. It follows that many clients who may appear angry or aggressive often do so as a result of what they regard as poor service or of being treated badly by the company in question.

Yet good customer service is important in dealing with the clients of any company, regardless of whether you work in a service industry or in manufacturing. Put yourself in your clients' shoes and ask yourself how you would respond in their situation. If they have encountered bad or inefficient service, don't they have a right to complain? And if they do feel that way about the company, then to whom are they going to make their feelings known? Why, to you, the frontline staff, of course. So there is no point in taking their abuse personally.

Often, it is extremely stressful to be harangued by an angry client. Keeping calm really is the only way to deal with such people because if you become irate as a result of how he talks to you, then absolutely nothing will be achieved, and his current perceptions of you and your company will only be reinforced. The logical consequence of this is that he may never come back for a second time, and worse still, he may bad-mouth your company to all his friends, thus ensuring that they never use your services either.

People don't get angry for no reason, and dissatisfied clients are usually angry for only a small number of possible reasons. Perhaps they feel that:

● no one appears to want to listen to them, or to take their complaints seriously
● the product they purchased does not work in the way it should
● they are not getting the help they require
● their expectations have not been met
● the company is not taking their complaint as seriously as they are.

In all of these cases, it is necessary to show them that you take what they are saying seriously. And that means listening, and showing them that you are not only listening but also taking notice. Take time to take in a few deep breaths, and try to relax your posture. If you are tensed up, you can never hide that fact from the other person.

Body language is very useful in this situation, as is paraphrasing what they have said to show that you have absorbed the essence of their concerns. By asking questions to learn more about their complaint, you will get to the heart of the problem more quickly.

In dealing with angry clients, you should also attempt to empathize with them. At the start of your conversation, you are unlikely to know whether they have good cause to be upset. Try putting yourself in their position, listening carefully, maintaining eye contact and generally getting on the same wavelength. In this way you can demonstrate to them that there is no question of it being a situation of them against your company, but rather that you are on their side to try to sort out the issue.

Once you have dealt with getting their feelings back on an even keel, you should set about dealing with the problem itself. One of the most powerful things anyone can do in such a situation is to ask directly 'What can I do to help?'

When dealing with a difficult customer or client, it is no good saying you cannot solve their complaint. At the very least you will need to offer some alternative solutions so that you are seen to be making an effort to get somewhere close to finding the answer to their problem.

Give your client at least two alternative solutions so that in effect you are giving him the option of taking control of the solution once again. Sometimes there may be no options for you even to offer, in which case you should explain why it is impossible to accede to his wishes. However, you should still do all you can to come up with some acceptable solution so that he can see that you are genuinely trying to help, and not to give him the brush-off.

How to deal with a face-to-face complaint

1 As soon as it becomes obvious that you will have to deal with an angry client or customer with a complaint, take a few deep breaths and try to relax.

2 Remain calm at all times and take an assertive stance, showing him that you are unfazed by his temper.

3 Try to see the situation from his point of view and empathize wherever possible with his predicament.

4 Listen, question and paraphrase wherever possible in order to demonstrate that you really do understand the problem.

5 Find out what, if any, his solution would be to the problem.

6 Offer a solution – if at all possible, incorporate his suggestions; if not, attempt to create a solution acceptable to both parties.

The last thing you should do is to offer excuses as to why something has not been done. Frankly, the customer does not wish to know whose fault it was. As far as he is concerned, you are the public face of the company and it is the company that is at fault; therefore, by a logical extension, you are at fault. The most important thing is to get whatever was wrong put right. Once you have decided what must be done, explain what you intend to him and then make sure that you actually do it.

Complaints over the telephone, email and other electronic media can add further complications to finding a solution, for it is an unfortunate fact that many people, who would not dream of being rude to anyone directly, become much more aggressive where no facial contact is taking place. And because there is no non-verbal feedback going on – i.e. the facial expressions and the hand movements that we all take for granted in normal conversation – some people are altogether less coherent when talking over the phone.

How many times, also, have you been put on hold for an eternity by a not-very-bright receptionist and then put through to someone who is unable to help you anyway? It happens to all of us, and the worst part about it is not knowing what is happening at the other end of the line. Have they forgotten us? Do they care? Does anyone want to help us solve the problem? Would we be better off taking our business elsewhere?

This is why dealing with complainants over the telephone can often become even more stressful than facing the wrath of a difficult customer eyeball to eyeball. But equally, it is even more essential that you remain cool, calm and collected when dealing with such a person over the wires. Without the feedback inherent in body language, it is very important to give verbal feedback to the complainant that you are not only still listening to him, but also understand his problems and wish to help him find a solution to them.

How to deal with complaints over the phone

1 Always have a notepad or screen beside you so that you can note down the complaints; there could be more than one, after all!

2 Make sure that, if you cannot find a solution there and then, you say that you will get back to him at a later time – and make sure you do!

3 If you are unable to resolve the problem yourself, explain why and that you will ask the relevant person to ring him back.

4 Make sure that you have all his relevant details – name, telephone number and address, and the reason why he called you in the first place.

Threatening behaviour

Unfortunately, there are sometimes occasions when the level of frustration or anger of the client reaches boiling point and he starts to swear or exhibit threatening behaviour. What should you do in such circumstances? There is a school of thought that says that no one should have to put up with threatening or abusive language, and that in such a situation you should either put the phone down on the complainant or, in a person-to-person situation, simply walk away. Unfortunately, life is not that easy. There are quite a few scenarios, such as dealing with patients and their relatives in hospitals, where it would obviously be quite inappropriate to absolve oneself of their problems when they are emotionally charged up. Equally, however, no one should normally have to be on the receiving end of such behaviour, and it is best if you are likely to find yourself in such a position that you discuss what the company's policy is on such matters before it actually happens.

It could also be a very good idea to see what it is that is making the clients unhappy with your service. Have you, for instance, given them expectations that cannot be met? Do you know what promises your salespeople are making? Is the competition giving better service or better-quality products for the same price? If so, a proper review of your place in the market may well reduce the number of 'difficult people' you have to deal with altogether.

Summary

When it is necessary to say no to a request, we may face several difficulties, not least in the way this makes us feel about ourselves. We want to avoid confrontation, to be helpful and to be popular – particularly with the boss. However, there are many occasions when 'No' is the only honest and realistic answer and there are constructive ways of saying this.

In an effort to avoid causing displeasure by not refusing to take something on, we are more likely to compound the problem at a later date. In contrast, by being politely assertive and explaining why you are unable to help on this occasion, you are more likely to gain respect and be viewed positively. Harder still than saying no to a boss or colleague is saying it to a client, but there are times, too, when this is appropriate. Remaining calm and polite is, of course, essential, as is showing the client that you are treating their complaint seriously, listening and taking notice, explaining what you intend to do and then doing it. It is important not to be easily offended, intimidated or provoked into an angry response.

SUNDAY
MONDAY
TUESDAY
WEDNESDAY
THURSDAY
FRIDAY
SATURDAY

Fact-check (answers at the back)

Some of these questions have more than one correct answer.

1. Why do many of us dislike saying no?
   a) We want to avoid confrontation ❏
   b) We want to be liked ❏
   c) We want to be helpful ❏
   d) We like to feel we are being taken advantage of ❏

2. Saying yes at work, when we should have said no, can cause which of the following problems?
   a) You might ultimately not produce work of the required standard ❏
   b) You might become inefficient and late through an excessive workload ❏
   c) Your colleagues will see you as being too helpful ❏
   d) It gives the wrong feedback on your workload ❏

3. How do you say no assertively?
   a) By being aggressive, so it is clear you are not open to persuasion ❏
   b) By explaining why you cannot or will not do something ❏
   c) By making excuses ❏
   d) By telling lies if necessary ❏

4. What are the likely outcomes of being irate with an angry client?
   a) Impressing them with the strength of your belief in your company ❏
   b) Reinforcing their current perceptions of you and the company ❏
   c) They may 'bad-mouth' your company to their contacts ❏
   d) They may not return for repeat business ❏

5. Which of the following are usual reasons for a client to feel angry?
   a) You have exceeded their expectations ❏
   b) No one appears to want to take them seriously ❏
   c) The product they purchased is not working as they thought it would ❏
   d) They are not getting the service they require ❏

6. Which of the following are good ways of responding to an angry client?
   a) Attempting to empathize with them ❏
   b) Mirroring them; if they shout, you shout, if they are calm, so are you ❏
   c) Listening carefully, to establish if they have good cause to be upset ❏
   d) Reassuring them that you wish to sort the situation out ❏

7. Which of the following are good methods for dealing with the client's problem?
a) Offer excuses why something has not been done ❏
b) Tell them whose fault it is ❏
c) If there are no options available for you to offer, explain that this is the case ❏
d) Ask directly, 'What can I do to help?' ❏

8. Which of the following apply when dealing with a difficult person in a telephone call?
a) They are less likely to be rude or aggressive than in person ❏
b) It can be more stressful than a face-to-face interaction ❏
c) Verbal feedback is very important ❏
d) The lack of non-verbal feedback reduces the chance of a misunderstanding ❏

9. When dealing with a difficult person in a telephone call, what should you do?
a) Make sure that if you cannot offer an instant solution you will tell him that you will get back to him later ❏
b) Ensure you have an instant solution ❏
c) Take ownership of the problem ❏
d) If you are not the person to resolve the issue, explain that you will ask the relevant person to call him back ❏

10. What is the correct response to a client who starts to swear or exhibits threatening behaviour?
a) Always put the phone down, or walk away ❏
b) Inform the client of the company's policy on such matters, ideally before it actually happens ❏
c) Accept that, sometimes, dealing with such people is part of the job ❏
d) Remain calm but, if you feel unable to handle such interactions, consider changing jobs ❏

SATURDAY

You're in control now

Today we will draw together everything you have learned so far this week. We are reminded of the three basic character types of passive, aggressive and assertive. Assertiveness eliminates anxiety, expresses preferences and is not threatening, and is an area we should all work towards. We also revisit the need to understand ourselves, as this will enable us to work more effectively with others.

We are also reminded of the four main categories into which we can assign personality traits: insecure, negative, selfish and pleasant, and that we should honestly assess into which of these we fall. Conflict is reviewed, with stress avoidance being key to managing conflict. Positive and negative conflict may be experienced; it is the handling of the situation that determines how the conflict goes.

We remember that being positive is not the same as being a 'yes' person – there are times when it is appropriate and necessary to say no. All of this requires us to use our full communication skills, both verbal and non-verbal, to foster good and valuable relationships.

Understanding yourself

If we look back to Monday, and the general definitions of the three basic character types, we see that assertiveness means being able to act without anxiety or fear, while expressing our needs and preferences and not behaving in a hostile or threatening manner to others. It is the positive attitude towards the whole of the work and human relationships that can make the world go round, rather than punctuating life with a series of Mexican stand-offs or even a complete stalemate and abandonment of the plans and relationships involved.

As part of understanding that attitude, you have first to get to grips with understanding yourself and learning how to amend your behaviour and reactions to enable you to interact and work more effectively with others. Whatever your role in life, your understanding of where other people are coming from and why they are taking the stance they are takes you more than halfway to being able to energize your relationship with them and improve it in so many ways. If you apply this philosophy in your workplace as well, you will enable your colleagues to work with you much more effectively.

The first step, then, is to understand yourself, however uncomfortable that may make you feel. Coming face to face with yourself is not always a pleasure, but stick at it and make sure that you are not deluding yourself about any aspect of your own behaviour. You'll probably like yourself better afterwards, too!

We have all seen friends and acquaintances deluding themselves on a daily basis, such as when:

● they only tell 'white' lies when they amend their CVs in order to change the substance of their recorded personal history
● they think that they are quiet, shy and retiring, when they are truly gregarious and tend to show off!
● they say they are 'on a diet' when, in reality, they snack all day.

We are usually our own worst enemies in life anyway, and we are always sad to see friends who labour away under a damaging false premise – but how many of us are actually brave enough to grasp the nettle and tell them? Indeed, should we tell them at all?

It is a truism that many of us are the products of our own upbringing. We saw on Tuesday that although there are many different types of personality trait, the four main categories can be broken down into *insecure*, *negative*, *selfish* and *pleasant*. We would all like to see ourselves in the fourth camp, but the reality might be very different.

Then there is the knottiest problem of all – why are particular people a problem to us anyway? What is it that they do or say that really gets our goat? Are we the real problem here, after all?

Questions to ask yourself

You need to ask yourself these questions – or slightly milder versions of them – whenever a new situation arises or a potential conflict scenario appears to be looming up to overshadow your relationships and work.

- How do others see me?
- How can I find out truthfully how others see me?
- Has the experience of childhood left its scar on me for life?
- How much of the negativity from that scar can I overcome?
- Have I really learned that others have needs too?
- Do I take these into account when I am speaking to others?
- Can I better myself and help others with similar problems?
- How can I best develop myself to do that?

Managing conflict and reducing stress

Conflict is the spice of life and arises in all kinds of everyday situations, but it has to be emphasized that not all conflict is bad. Your managing the conflict in your life is the key to avoiding stress, and so the perception of what it is that is causing the conflict in the first place is well worth achieving. Put succinctly, conflict can be either positive or negative. By positive conflict, we mean a situation in which the generation of enthusiasm can be the catalyst to solving a problem that up till now has remained stubbornly impenetrable. Negative conflict, on the other hand, can lead both to stress and to the failure of the two parties to come to any kind of agreement.

The key is to find common ground and attempt to see things from the other person's point of view. That doesn't necessarily mean he is right – only that his opinion should not be dismissed out of hand; it is perfectly possible to see things from a number of different angles, each one of which may well be valid. You may know the story of the three blind men stumbling across an elephant. One came across its trunk, while the second was fanned by one of its ears. The third walked into one of its massive legs. Who gave the best description of this animal? Would the blind man who described a snake-like creature be any more wrong – or right – than the one who had experienced a downdraught from a giant fan, or the other who thought he had discovered a giant tree trunk?

Staying positive

Being negative and putting a dampener on things is all too easy. Everyone gets depressed at times, but inevitably it is the positive people in society who get things moving and who win in the end. So if, in addition to being positive in your own right, you get others to behave positively to you too, then it follows that you are much more likely to find a way forward in all aspects of your life.

But what do we mean by being positive? It certainly is not the same as being a 'yes' person. Being positive means looking for a way forward through a difficult situation, looking for the good things and working out how to improve the bad. Sometimes that is simply a matter of improving your communication skills in order to give feedback to your opposite number. Being able to interpret non-verbal signals and to back up your own conversation with the appropriate body language are also skills that are well worth developing in order to avoid misunderstandings.

Equally, many people experience great difficulty when finding themselves in a situation where they have to say no to someone. None of us likes doing it, because it is against basic human nature. But being able to say no is an important weapon in our armoury of techniques for being more open and honest with our colleagues. It isn't easy; no one ever said it was. But by tackling the difficult situation head-on, you are less likely to store up further problems in the future, and equally you will end up better respected by your colleagues, who will see you as a straight-dealing type of person to be working with!

At the end of the day, good communication is at the very heart of dealing with difficult people. Many people can be exasperating, and there are times when we all wonder whether there is any point in putting up with their general behaviour and attitudes. Yet, give in to the temptation of treating like with like and who wins in the end? You don't, because you will soon see that by behaving like your opposite number you have actually sunk to his level. He doesn't either, because for a start he has lost your respect and most likely the respect of others around you.

SUNDAY
MONDAY
TUESDAY
WEDNESDAY
THURSDAY
FRIDAY
SATURDAY

TIP *It is worth remembering an old adage that goes something along the lines of 'When you point an accusing finger at somebody, you should watch out as there are always three fingers that are pointing back at you!'*

Without sounding awfully 'goody goody', assertive behaviour and setting a good example can be an inspiration to others. On the other hand, following their lead and behaving badly, giving others a difficult time, can never lead to a positive outcome. Perhaps Charles Kingsley, in his famous novel *The Water Babies*, summed up the situation perfectly with his two characters Mrs 'Do-as-you-would-be-done-by' and Mrs 'Be-done-by-as-you-did'.

So get positive, try to see the other person's point of view and, above all, communicate, and hopefully other people will soon stop being difficult in your company and will perhaps surprise even themselves. Surely that has to be a good thing?

Summary

Over the past week we have seen that the key to dealing with difficult people is to be found within ourselves. When we know and understand ourselves, we are better able to control our own behaviour and, by the way we conduct ourselves, guide the responses of others in our interactions with them.

From what we have learned of the different types of behaviour – passive, aggressive and assertive – the different behavioural patterns – insecure, negative, selfish and pleasant – and the different personality types – dictatorial, enthusiastic, empathetic and processor – we can anticipate the potential reactions of others and begin the process of enabling them to react differently. This gives us a good chance of managing conflict situations so they are positive, facilitated by our communication skills and body language.

We have learned that by moving ourselves as much into assertiveness as possible, when necessary we will be able to say no to our colleagues, boss and even clients, in a constructive manner. Through all of this, we can learn to deal with difficult people – who may suddenly start to become less difficult.

SUNDAY
MONDAY
TUESDAY
WEDNESDAY
THURSDAY
FRIDAY
SATURDAY

Fact-check [answers at the back]

Some of these questions have more than one correct answer.

1. When responding to difficult people, what should we do?
   a) Not get angry; it's a harmful way of reacting ❑
   b) Not stand up to them ❑
   c) Make excuses and be defensive ❑
   d) Get angry; it's the only appropriate reaction ❑

2. What does assertiveness mean?
   a) Being able to act without anxiety or fear ❑
   b) Expressing our needs and preferences without behaving in a threatening manner to others ❑
   c) A positive attitude to work and human relationships ❑
   d) Sometimes accepting that the easy option is to go along with someone else, even if we don't agree with them ❑

3. Conflict is the spice of life and arises in all kinds of everyday situations. What else is true of conflict?
   a) The way you manage it is key to avoiding stress ❑
   b) It is always negative ❑
   c) It may be useful in solving a problem ❑
   d) What caused it in the first place is irrelevant; how you resolve it is the only thing that matters ❑

4. In conflict resolution, what should we do?
   a) Assume the other person is always right; it is the only way to resolve an issue ❑
   b) Attempt to see things from the other person's point of view ❑
   c) Understand that there is only one correct solution ❑
   d) View the situation from a number of different angles, each one of which may well be valid ❑

5. What may feelings of negativity do?
   a) Cause you to see the worst in every situation ❑
   b) Cause others to see the negative aspects in you ❑
   c) Convey the best impression ❑
   d) Make a difficult situation worse ❑

6. What do we need to understand about our self-image?
   a) It may not match the image of us held by others ❑
   b) It will inevitably match the image of us held by others ❑
   c) It is easy to criticize and improve upon ❑
   d) It is fixed and cannot be altered ❑

7. What will improving your self-image make you more likely to be able to do?
a) Resist the damaging words and actions of difficult people ❑
b) Gain a better insight into yourself ❑
c) Resist feeling hurt by a difficult person ❑
d) Never clash with a difficult person ❑

8. When can you really expect to influence others?
a) Only when you can see them as they are ❑
b) Only when you can see them as they would wish to be portrayed ❑
c) Only when you can see them as you wish they were ❑
d) Rarely; it is not really possible to influence others ❑

9. When considering the achievement of goals, which of the following statements apply?
a) Passive people rarely achieve their own goals because they rely on others to give them a lead instead of selecting their own ❑
b) Aggressive people often achieve their goals in the short term ❑
c) Aggressive people always achieve their goals ❑
d) Assertive people usually achieve their goals because in their view everyone can win ❑

10. What are the solutions to dealing with difficult people?
a) Avoiding difficult people in the first place ❑
b) Requiring us to see a mirror image of ourselves in others ❑
c) Controlling our own behaviour ❑
d) Seeing the potential reactions of others in order to enable them to react differently ❑

SUNDAY
MONDAY
TUESDAY
WEDNESDAY
THURSDAY
FRIDAY
SATURDAY

7 × 7

1 Seven things to do today

- Make sure you are not the difficult person.
- Work out your approach to your colleagues on the job in hand.
- Before complaining about the attitude of others, think about how they view you.
- Smile and think positively before opening your mouth.
- Schedule in some 'head space'.
- At the end of the day, plan for tomorrow.
- Celebrate something for someone else.

2 Seven key ideas

- When dealing with difficult people, always remember that it is about them and their problems. Be compassionate.
- When dealing with difficult people, remember that you cannot control their actions, only your own reactions to them.
- Dealing with difficult people may make us realize how much we need to work on our own character.
- Be thankful for all the difficult people in your life and learn from them. They have shown you exactly who you do not want to be.
- We are constantly being put to the test by trying circumstances, and difficult people and problems are not necessarily of our own making.
- Be confident in your own judgement of what is needed but do not be aggressive in putting it over.
- Try to think of difficult people as your teachers instead of your enemies.

3 Seven things to avoid

- Being unprepared for the strategy and tactics needed for the achievement of a project
- Repeating the errors of yesterday in how you handle other people
- Working against people who are on the same side
- Being overwhelmed and therefore disorganized
- Letting people down
- Being disrespectful
- Being late

4 Seven ways to respond to difficult behaviour

- Being confrontational demonstrates the ultimate in pushy and aggressive behaviour. You need to send a clear signal that you are strong and capable, since anything less is an invitation for further attack.
- Covert complaining tries to make you look bad or undermine you. Once you have exposed their position, it becomes useless.
- Know-it-all behaviour has a low tolerance for error. Think through your ideas ahead of time since the person adopting this behaviour monitors all incoming information for errors and will pick up any shortcomings to discredit your whole idea.
- Some people explode into unfocused ranting and raving after a period of calm about things that have nothing to do with the present circumstances. Don't try to have a discussion with a person behaving in this way. Have a break for ten minutes before having a follow-up meeting.
- In an effort to please people and avoid confrontation, 'yes people' say yes without thinking things through. Your goal with a person behaving like this is to get commitments you can count on by making it safe for that person to be honest and show that their contribution matters.

- A person exhibiting negative behaviour does not contribute to a conversation. The best kind of question to ask such a person is one that cannot be answered with a simple 'Yes' or 'No'. Use questions that begin with the words, 'Who', 'What', 'When', 'Where' or 'How', since they tend to open up topics for discussion.
- People who cannot specify what they are unhappy with frequently prefer to sidestep the issue, postpone a solution or make vague generalizations. Encourage this person to take a gentle approach to the issue in order to understand the specific components of the problem and come to a solution.

5 Seven aspects of body language

- Facial expressions can convey many different emotions and are among the most universal forms of body language. In some cases, our facial expressions may reveal our true feelings about a particular situation. While you may say that you are feeling fine, the look on your face may suggest otherwise.
- How we stand and hold our bodies also tells a story. Posture conveys a wealth of information, not just about a physical condition but how a person is feeling, such as whether they are confident, open or submissive.
- The strength and confidence of the handshake can tell you a lot about the person. Studies have demonstrated several handshake styles, e.g. the finger squeeze, the bone-crusher, the limp fish, etc. Handshakes are popular in the US and are appropriate for use between men and women. However, in Muslim and Hindu cultures people do not shake hands.
- The eyes are frequently referred to as 'the windows of the soul', since they are capable of revealing a great deal about what a person is feeling or thinking. As you engage in conversation with another person, taking note of eye movements is a natural and important part of the communication process. You might also note whether people are making direct eye contact or averting their gaze, how much they're blinking and whether their pupils are dilated.

- Mouth expressions and movements can also be essential in reading body language. For example, chewing the bottom lip may indicate that the individual is experiencing worry, fear or insecurity. Covering the mouth may be an effort to be polite (if the person is yawning or coughing) but it may also be an attempt to cover up a sneer of disapproval.
- Gestures can be some of the most direct and obvious body language signals. Waving, pointing and using the fingers to indicate numerical amounts are all very common and easy-to-understand gestures. Some gestures may be culturally specific. Giving the thumbs-up or the 'peace' sign may have completely different connotations in different parts of the world.
- Arms and legs can be useful in conveying non-verbal information. Crossing the arms can indicate defensiveness. Crossing legs away from another person may indicate dislike or discomfort with that individual, as does turning away from the person. Other subtle signals such as spreading the arms widely may be an attempt to seem larger and more commanding, while keeping the arms close to the body may be an effort to minimize oneself or withdraw from attention.

6 Seven of the best quotes

- 'Great leadership does not mean running away from reality. Sometimes the hard truths might just demoralize the company, but at other times sharing difficulties can inspire people to take action that will make the situation better.' John Kotter
- 'Each of us is leading a difficult life, and when we meet people we are seeing only a tiny part of the thinnest veneer of their complex, troubled existences. To practise anything other than kindness to them, to treat them in any way save generously, is to quietly deny their humanity.' Derren Brown
- 'So much of what we call management consists in making it difficult for people to work.' Peter F. Drucker
- 'Courage is fire, and bullying is smoke.' Benjamin Disraeli

- 'If you're going to be two-faced, at least make one of them pretty.' Marilyn Monroe
- 'Some people won't be happy until they've pushed you to the ground. What you have to do is have the courage to stand your ground and not give them the time of day. Hold on to your power and never give it away.' Donna Schoenrock
- 'Difficult people are your key to self-empowerment; you need to learn how to cope with them, not let them dominate and affect you.' Janice Davies

7 Seven of the best resources

- *Who Moved My Cheese?* by Dr Spencer Johnson (Vermilion, 1999)
- *S.U.M.O.* by Paul McGee (Capstone, 2015)
- *Managing Yourself in A Week* by Martin Manser (Teach Yourself, 2016)
- *The Naked Leader* by David Taylor (Bantam, 2003)
- *Inside Organizations* by Charles Handy (BBC Books, 1990)
- *Mind Gym* by Sebastian Bailey & Octavius Black (HarperCollins, 2014)
- *The Definitive Book of Body Language* by Allan & Barbara Pease (Orion, 2006)

Answers

Sunday: 1b,d; 2c; 3a,d; 4d; 5a,b,c;
6c,d; 7a,b,d; 8c,d; 9a,b,c; 10b,d

Monday: 1b,c,d; 2a,b,d; 3b,c,d;
4b,d; 5a,c; 6a,b,c; 7b,c,d;
8a,b,c; 9b,c,d; 10a,c,d

Tuesday: 1a,b,c; 2b; 3a,c,d;
4a,b,d; 5a,b,c; 6c,d; 7a,b; 8c,d;
9b,c,d; 10a,c

Wednesday: 1c; 2a,c; 3b,d; 4d;
5c; 6a,b,c; 7a,b,d; 8a,c,d;
9b,c,d; 10a,d

Thursday: 1b,c; 2b,c,d; 3c,d;
4b,d; 5c,d; 6a,b,c; 7a,b,d;
8a,c,d; 9b,c,d; 10b,c,d

Friday: 1a,b,c; 2a,b,d; 3b; 4b,c,d;
5b,c,d; 6a,c,d; 7c,d; 8b,c; 9a,d;
10b,c,d

Saturday: 1a; 2a,b,c; 3a,c; 4b,d;
5a,b,d; 6a; 7a,b,c; 8a; 9a,b,d;
10b,c,d

ALSO AVAILABLE IN THE 'IN A WEEK' SERIES

APPRAISALS • BRAND MANAGEMENT • BUSINESS PLANS • CONTENT MARKETING • COVER LETTERS • DIGITAL MARKETING • DIRECT MARKETING • EMOTIONAL INTELLIGENCE • FINDING & HIRING TALENT • JOB HUNTING • LEADING TEAMS • MARKET RESEARCH • MARKETING • MBA • MOBILE MARKETING • NETWORKING • OUTSTANDING CONFIDENCE • PEOPLE MANAGEMENT • PLANNING YOUR CAREER • PROJECT MANAGEMENT • SMALL BUSINESS MARKETING • STARTING A NEW JOB • TACKLING TOUGH INTERVIEW QUESTIONS • TIME MANAGEMENT

For information about other titles in the 'In A Week' series, please visit
www.teachyourself.co.uk